# *The* POINT *of* VIABILITY

# Praise for *The Point of Viability*

*The Point of Viability: A Coming Alive Story* is a tender and courageous witness to the kind of joy that does not deny suffering, but grows alongside it. Julie Yost invites us into the sacred tension of profound loss and fierce hope. Her story reveals a joy that is neither naïve nor forced, but deeply incarnational.

With honesty and reverence, Julie shows us that grief and gratitude are not opposites, but companions. She offers no platitudes—only presence. No easy answers—only a faithful attentiveness to the moment God has given. In the long days of bedrest, uncertainty, and heartbreak, she discovers that joy is not found by escaping pain, but by fully inhabiting it with love.

This book will resonate deeply with parents who have carried loss in their bodies and hearts, and with anyone who has learned that waiting can be holy ground. *The Point of Viability* is a beautiful reminder that even in the most fragile spaces of loss and uncertainty, God still meets us—and life, in all its tenderness, can still come alive.

—**Kelly Breaux**, Author of *Hiding in the Upper Room: How the Catholic Sacraments Healed Me from Child Loss* and Founder of Red Bird Ministries

I'm blown away by this book! Julie writes with such honesty and grace as she shares her journey with infertility, a challenging pregnancy, loss, miracles, God's healing love, and the joy of life. As a marriage and family therapist—and through my wife and sister, both Labor and Delivery nurses—I've heard similar gripping stories. But through Julie's gifted writing, I experienced these realities even more intimately. As I read, I felt like I was sharing in every woman's suffering and joy. I cried and praised God for his goodness in each moving chapter and in Julie's vulnerable and faith-filled reflections. I have always admired holy women, but my admiration grew by leaps and bounds through Julie's account.

—**Dr. Bob Schuchts**, Bestselling Author of
*Be Healed*—and other notable books—and
Founder of John Paul II Healing Center

A profound story of how Jesus Christ can draw good even out of our most painful experiences. If you want to witness the birth of our crucified and risen Lord within a soul, read this book. As a priest who meets with women and men grieving the loss of a child, I will be buying this book in bulk to assure them they are not alone.

—**Father Eric Roush**, Catholic Priest in Cincinnati

A story brimming with the sacredness and beauty of life—however brief—and the power of prayer, *The Point of Viability* reminds readers that the Author of Life always writes a riveting story. Julie Yost reveals with tenderness and transparency her journey of pregnancy, hope, loss, and love. Even more, she offers readers the opportunity to reflect on and pray through their own sacred stories. A triumph of trust in God's mysterious provision!

—**Claire Dwyer**, Author of *This Present Paradise:*
*A Spiritual Journey with St. Elizabeth of the Trinity*
and Co-Founder of Write These Words

Sacred scripture proclaims that motherhood is, by its very essence, salvific (1 Tim 2:15). In *The Point of Viability*, author Julie Yost offers a compelling and vulnerable glimpse into the cross she suffered in her motherhood and the new life she found in Christ. This captivating story is a story every mother must read. Every ounce of Yost's heart is poured out on these pages as a promise of hope.

—**Carrie Daunt**, Author of *Undone: Freeing your Feminine Heart from the Knots of Fear and Shame* and Co-Author of *Man Your Post: Learning to Lead like St. Joseph*

*The Point of Viability: A Coming Alive Story* beautifully shows how to incorporate faith even in the most difficult seasons of life. Julie shares her journey through a high-risk pregnancy, revealing both the joys and the sorrows of growing new life within her. The book will leave you inspired.

—**Emily Jaminet**, prolific and award-winning Author, Speaker, Radio Personality, and Executive Director of the Sacred Heart Enthronement Network and Co-Founder of Inspire the Faith.

*The Point of Viability: A Coming Alive Story* is an inspiring and deeply moving pro-life testimony that invites prayerful reflection on God's presence amid suffering and uncertainty. Through one mother's courageous trust in divine providence during a high-risk pregnancy, her story reveals how faith transforms fear into hope and hardship into grace. It's a powerful reminder of God's tender intervention in the most fragile moments of life and a call to recognize His hand in the challenges and joys that shape our own journeys.

—**Bob Wurzelbacher**, Director of Respect Life Ministries for the Archdiocese of Cincinnati

In *The Point of Viability,* Julie Yost gives us a raw and tender passageway into one of life's most beautiful and vulnerable experiences — maternity. Through her journey of inexplicable suffering, trust, and surrender, Julie invites readers into the most sacred spaces of her story. One cannot read through the pages of this book without being moved to tears in the most beautiful and Christ-centered way. The hope that abounds through her physical, maternal, and spiritual journey leaves readers with a renewed desire to entrust all things to God's providence. Thank you, Julie, for welcoming us into these sacred corners of a mother's heart.

—**Suzanne Bilodeau**, Author of *She Loved: Resting in the Beauty of Motherhood* and Creator and Host of the *Latte & Laundry Podcast*

# *The* POINT *of* VIABILITY

*A Coming Alive Story*

JULIE YOST

Cover design by Caroline Green

Cover photo by Christina Shchodra / Shutterstock

ISBN: 978-1-5051-3863-4
ePUB ISBN: 978-1-5051-4078-1

Published in the United States by
Good & True Media
PO Box 269
Gastonia, NC 28053
www.GoodAndTrueMedia.com

Printed in India

To my best friend, Dave,
and to my beloved children here on earth
and the ones I love and miss in heaven—
Johnny, Emma, Charlie, and Grace.
Through each of you,
I have known the presence of God.

And to all who have endured
profound suffering and loss—
may you know the hope, healing,
and abundant life found in Jesus.

# Contents

INTRODUCTION

# On the Cross

IT HAPPENED so fast. The nurse checked me and shockingly announced that baby A's head was coming out right now and that we had to get to the OR, STAT! What happened next reminded me of a scene from a medical show on TV. Several nurses rushed into my room and loaded me on a gurney. They ran alongside my stretcher down a long hallway, holding on to IV bags, machines, and the handles of my bed as they emphatically told me not to push. My husband, Dave, said later that as they were running, they gave me a mega dose of the "Mag"—the medicine to stop the contractions—nearly four times the amount they'd ever given me before. It did nothing. Dave ran alongside my bed on wheels trying to keep up with the nurses and this sudden turn of events.

The contractions came so hard and so fast that I let out a stream of loud, guttural cries. I'm not usually a yeller, but this force of nature was much too strong for me to contain myself. All measures of poise and control went out the window at this point. The nurses kept telling me not to push, but the gravitational force was too great for me not to comply with its wishes. As we burst into the operating room, they prepped the area for an emergency C-section while various people shouted orders to one another in the room.

In a matter of seconds, in between contractions that were literally moments apart, the nurses managed to sit me up and administer an epidural in my spine. As I was laid back down on the operating table, I became aware of the flurry of activity and nervous energy all around. There were literally twenty or so experts in the field of neonatology gathering to prepare to transport my three extremely premature babies to the NICU immediately after birth. As they flurried about in multiple directions around my bed, some tried to soothe me with comforting words like, "You're doing great," and "The babies will be here soon," while others gave me instructions on what was going to happen next.

As the nurses and doctors were getting prepped for surgery, I was told to stretch out my arms in a T-formation on the table. Then they tied my wrists down with straps so I wouldn't have the urge to sit up during the surgery. After that, they put a small curtain up so I couldn't see as they cut into my flesh to quickly extract the babies.

This surgery needed to happen quickly so the babies wouldn't be in any more distress. Medical professionals whisked around me in their scrubs, hats, and masks, while the epidural started kicking in. I was in a state of shock. The words of the specialists jumbled together, along with the noises of machines humming in the background. I gradually began to notice the subliminal weight of someone staring at me. As blurred bodies swirled around, I slowly turned my head in the direction of the stare and saw a masked figure coming toward me, fully gowned up like the rest of the people buzzing around my bed. He came close, got down on his knees, and looked intently at me. I didn't recognize who he was at first, as most of his face and head were covered. But as a teardrop fell from his eye and he clasped my hand, I knew. It was my husband, Dave. He had just been allowed entry into the surgery room. He looked at me with the most loving and kind eyes imaginable, and as he witnessed me with arms outstretched and about to be cut open to deliver his precious children, he spoke to me in the softest and most gentle voice and said, "It looks like you're on the cross."

I was.

## CHAPTER 1

# Roses

*"Ask and it will be given to you; seek and you will find; knock and the door will be opened to you."*

—Mt 7:7

I WAS looking for a miracle. My son Johnny was two, and my husband Dave and I were struggling to conceive another child. We desperately wanted another baby, as we'd always hoped for at least two children in our family.

At that time, I had a condition called PCOS (Polycystic Ovarian Syndrome). This meant I couldn't have a menstrual cycle without the help of some medication. Knowing this, Dave and I knew we'd need some extra help when trying to have children. We decided early on that we'd only consider fertility treatments that aligned with our Catholic faith tradition. We weren't going to do invasive procedures like in-vitro fertilization or artificial insemination to conceive a child. We limited our actions to a specific medication formulated to help my body to ovulate, and then we'd try to have a baby the "old-fashioned way". This method worked great on our first attempt with our first baby, so we naturally thought it would work again. This would prove not to be the case.

During each cycle of treatment, I was given a series of ten to twelve subcutaneous shots to stimulate my ovaries and induce ovulation. Sometimes the shots were in my hip, and other times they'd be in my abdomen. I'd drive to the doctor's office during this process every three or four days so they could check on the progress of what was happening internally. When the timing seemed just right, I'd get one more shot with a different medication that would stimulate the release of an egg. Finally, a couple of days later, my husband and I would get to the fun part of the process in hopes that pregnancy would result.

At this point in time, we had undergone five cycles of this treatment, which in reality meant almost a year of hell. The shots in my abdomen were incredibly painful, my hormones were supercharged and out of control, there were constant doctor's appointments to monitor how things were going, and the torment of not being pregnant month after month in spite of all these efforts was taking its toll. My hope and my patience were diminishing, and I felt as though I could hardly tolerate any more.

I remember sitting in our master bathroom one evening, preparing to get another shot in my stomach. I couldn't bear the thought of puncturing myself with a sharp object, though I admit to trying several times, only to stop right before the needle pierced my skin. Because of my inability to give myself the shots, my husband agreed early on to do the honors instead. Luckily, he is a pharmacist and was comfortable with the idea.

Usually when Dave did this, I'd sit on the edge of our whirlpool tub on the cold white tiles and then mentally prepare myself for a couple minutes in order to willingly become a human pincushion. Each time, I had to give myself a pep talk so I would have the courage to let another human being stab my stomach with a pointed object. I'm usually not that needle-shy either because I got regular allergy shots as a kid and was totally okay with it. But those shots were in my arm . . . and in the doctor's office . . . and given by a certified nurse. Shots to my stomach administered by my husband were a whole different ballgame altogether!

On this particular night, I mustered up the courage to slowly lift my shirt once again to expose my belly for yet another painful injection. There were fresh bruises from the last few nights of shots. As I looked into my husband's sensitive, baby blue eyes, I tried to garner the strength to let him give me another shot. This time, though, I simply couldn't. A surge of exhaustion, discouragement, and hopelessness welled up inside of me and bubbled over. I had reached my limit and just could not take an ounce more of this self-inflicted pain.

Tears trickled down my cheeks as I was suddenly faced with a new and harsh reality. This clearly was not working, and we couldn't keep doing this indefinitely. That night I took a harrowing look at the fact that at some point if this continued to fail, we would eventually have to stop the treatment and give up on our dream of having more of our own biological children. This was a reality I'd never before had to come to terms with, but one that surfaced with a soul-crushing force. The truth of the matter was that this was becoming too much to bear both physically and emotionally. After letting all of this out, I finally allowed Dave to give me the last shot of this round of treatment. We knew we'd have a lot of difficult conversations ahead.

Over the next few days, my husband and I had many heated discussions and shed many tears as we decided what we wanted to do as a couple. Together, we came to the heart-wrenching decision that this would be our last month of trying to conceive another child with medication. We just couldn't continue to live like this, day in and day out, for months on end. Despite the fact that we desperately wanted to have another child to complete our family, it had become too much for us. Our hopes for a second baby were slipping away. . . .

It was an interesting coincidence, then, that during this last month of medically trying to become pregnant, I found myself in the Rose Chapel of our church with our high school youth group at a meeting called "Miracles." I was a regular volunteer with the teens in our robust youth ministry program that year. The student leaders, alongside adult helpers, led meetings among their peers. The team of leaders responsible for the activities of this night decided they were going to have a meeting on miracles, and I was excited! I wasn't part of this planning team, so I didn't know what was in store on this Sunday evening.

As the meeting unfolded, I found myself on the edge of my seat as I sat and listened to a few of our student ministers tell stories of God's incredible miracles they had witnessed in their short lifetimes. One spirit-filled young lady's testimony touched me to the core. Her name was Liz, and she shared the story of how her aunt was cured of cancer.

The doctors told Liz's aunt that she only had a few months to live. Liz's family, being devout Catholics, began to recite a prayer called a novena to elicit help from Saint Thérèse of Lisieux. I like to describe asking a saint to intercede for you like asking a heavenly friend to pray for you, much like you would ask a friend to pray for you here on earth. The only difference is that the saints are in heaven and much closer to God!

St. Thérèse is known the world over as "The Little Flower" for doing small, ordinary things with extraordinary love. She lived in the 1800s in France and became a devout nun as a teenager. She had incredible mystical experiences of Jesus and Mary and wrote down many of her revelations from God. Thérèse ended up suffering from tuberculosis and lived only twenty-four short years.

Before her death, Thérèse prophetically predicted that her mission would truly begin after she died. She sensed that in heaven she would let a shower of roses fall upon the earth that would be God's gifts for humankind. Ever since her passing, miracles have happened for many who have sought her aid. After asking for her intercessory prayers, people have reported being cured of all sorts of ailments and conditions. Word began to spread about this young girl from Lisieux and her heavenly influence. People around the world began to recognize Thérèse's holiness, and in time she was canonized by the Catholic Church and became an official saint.

This is the saint to whom my young friend Liz in the youth group turned for help. Liz carefully followed the instructions of a novena where she said certain prayers on several consecutive days asking Saint Thérèse to appeal to God for her specific request. Novenas are typically nine days of prayer for a specific intention, but this one was five. Liz prayed the first prayer, followed by her plea for help, and then prayed five Our Fathers, five Hail Marys, and five Glory Bes for five days straight, all before 11:00 a.m. On the fifth day, she was instructed to pray an additional five Our Fathers, Hail Marys, and Glory Bes. On the last day of the prayers, she was told that a rose would appear if God was to answer her prayer as requested. Honestly, this sounded a little hokey to me upon first hearing, but I continued to listen intently to my young friend's story.

After completing all the prayers as indicated with a sincerely faithful and expectant heart, Liz began looking for a rose that would indicate that God had heard and answered her prayers for her aunt to be healed. The day she said the last prayers of the novena, Liz went through her typical high school schedule and waited to see if she would receive a heavenly rose.

It is said that this rose could appear in any form—you could meet someone named Rose, you could receive some mail with a rose stamp on it, a random person could give you an actual rose, etc., so Liz was on the lookout. She went through her morning classes . . . first period, second, third . . . then fourth period, then lunch . . . not a rose in sight! But in fifth period, on this fifth day, Liz walked into her biology class. She looked around the room, and to her utter surprise, there was a picture on the wall she'd never seen before. It was a giant poster of a beautiful pink rose in full bloom, with drops of dew on each delicate petal! Liz immediately started grinning from ear to ear and had a sense that her aunt was going to be okay.

Liz sped home as fast as she could after school that day to call her aunt and tell her the story of the miraculous rose. She dialed her aunt's number. But before Liz could even get the words out, her aunt interrupted her. "Elizabeth, I've got great news—the cancer is gone!"

My heart just about burst out of my chest upon hearing this story in the midst of our youth group! I could hardly believe it! *This sort of thing actually works?*, I thought in amazement. *Even today? But here is a young lady standing right in front of me witnessing to the fact that it actually happened . . . and I know her family. She did not make this up!*

What a divine gift . . . and what impeccable timing! This was exactly what I needed to hear: a reminder that God is unbelievably powerful, that incredible miracles still happen today, and that this novena is a way in which I could pray for one. I left the meeting knowing I was going to try it.

I began saying the prescribed prayers the very next day. I prayed with all my might for another child since this was our last month of medically trying to conceive. I talked to Saint Thérèse out loud like she was my best friend, and I sincerely asked her to talk to Jesus—whom she loved and trusted so much—about my situation. I prayed the prayers just as I was supposed to until day five. I looked at the clock that day, and it read 11:21 a.m.

*Crap!*, I said to myself. *I missed the 11:00 a.m. requirement! I think I just screwed the whole thing up!* I reasoned, though, that God isn't legalistic and wouldn't mind if I was twenty-one minutes past the deadline. And anyway, it was 11:00 somewhere in the world, right?

It was the middle of winter on this special fifth day when I was to receive a mysterious rose if God was to grant me another child. This day was huge for me, and my two-year-old son Johnny and I anticipated how our rose would appear. I knew it would be difficult to receive a rose since it was snowing heavily, and I was pretty much in the house all day as a stay-at-home mom. I didn't want to cheat the divine system by going to a grocery store or something and just happen by a floral department. I put on my boots and coat and went out to check the mail. No letters with rose stamps. No bouquets delivered to the house. No calls from someone named Rose.

After my son Johnny's afternoon nap, as we were sharing a snack, he and I got into a deep conversation as you sometimes do with a two-year-old when you have no other adult interaction all day long.

"We're looking for a miracle today, Johnny," I said.

He said, "Me-a-kle," and then drank some juice from his sippy cup.

"Where are we going to find this miracle?" I asked him as I was heading for the sink.

Without skipping a beat, he clearly said, "Church," in his sweet little baby voice.

Astounded, I turned around and asked, "What did you say?"

Again, he matter-of-factly and pretty articulately said, "Church," while continuing to eat his Cheerios. My mind started racing, my pulse quickened . . . *Could the answer really be coming from the mouth of my small child?*

I knew in the depths of my soul that he was right. Of course that's where a miracle would be. We needed to go to church . . . right now! I yanked my boy out of his highchair and told him we were going on a little trip.

It was a snowy Friday afternoon around 3:00 p.m. as I bundled us both up to head to our church. As I was driving there, I thought, *The church is not going to be open at this hour on a Friday.* As I pulled into the frozen parking lot, my fears crystallized. There were no cars in the lot, and the church was dark. Still trusting my intuition and eager to get in, I pulled up next to the main entrance, put the car in park, and clumsily ran to give the doors a try. No such luck. They were all locked.

I peered inside the window of one of the front doors and happened to notice the custodian walking by with a vacuum just then. After I knocked a few times, he came over and opened the door a crack. I asked him if my son and I could go into the small Blessed Sacrament chapel for just a few minutes to pray. He agreed to let us in.

I excitedly clomped back to the car in my heavy boots, parked it in the lot, unbuckled Johnny from his car seat, trudged through the snow and ice, and went right through the main doors. I thanked the custodian again for letting us in and surveyed the main gathering area for roses. Not so much as a carnation. Then, hand in hand, Johnny and

I carefully made our way to the little chapel, and I slowly opened the door.

Once inside, the first thing I saw was a large bouquet of red roses! They were in a vase in the center of the room right underneath the beautifully carved wooden tabernacle. I instantly dropped to my knees and began sobbing. Tears of amazement poured down my cheeks, as I could hardly believe this was happening. A wave of awe and gratitude overtook me.

*Roses have appeared . . . on the fifth day . . . and to me?* I could hardly take it in as I knelt there surrounded by stained glass windows depicting various saints. Along with immense feelings of astonishment and thankfulness, I immediately had a keen sense of *knowing* deep in my being that I would have another child. This was the sign I'd been praying for. These roses were confirmation of an undeserved and beautiful gift of an answered prayer. In that moment, I was completely overwhelmed with God's love for me and the thought that He would grant me the miracle of new life!

Even more significant in the Catholic Church, the tabernacle in our Blessed Sacrament chapel is the sacred place where a consecrated host—the Eucharist—is kept. Catholics believe that when a Communion wafer has been blessed by a priest saying the exact same words that Jesus did at the Last Supper, Jesus becomes truly and fully alive and present to us—body, blood, soul, and divinity—disguised in this unique and humble form called the Holy Eucharist. God is able to do anything, from parting seas, to walking on water, to healing the sick. He comes to us in a myriad of ways to reach our hearts. The Eucharist is one of those beautiful and intimate ways. So, from my religious viewpoint and personal experience, these roses were literally located at the feet of Jesus, and the connection did not go unnoticed by me. Way to go, Saint Thérèse, bringing me right into the Lord's presence! I was beside myself to be touched by such grace!

As these connections were being made at a rapid-fire pace in my brain, a new batch of tears began to flow. All the while, Johnny frolicked about the chapel, unaware of my emotional outpouring or the prophetic role he played in this discovery. As I looked intently at the roses again, however, I began to notice something a bit strange about the flowers. They weren't full and robust and in perfect bloom like I'd imagined they'd be. The red petals were actually wilting a little and beginning to fade away. I plucked one petal off a single red rose in the vase, and I've saved it in my Bible to this day.

As Johnny and I left the little chapel and walked out again into the large gathering space, another peculiar thing happened. The TV monitor by the welcome desk flashed and said, "We're praying for the friends and family of Julie."

*That's weird,* I thought, *since my name is Julie.* I also observed by looking around that there had been a funeral there recently. The ecstatic joy of my answered prayer became tinged with a slight hint of dread. *Was God trying to temper my joy and caution me about this answered prayer? Would this pregnancy be difficult? Would I die during childbirth?*

All these thoughts swirled together in a whirlwind of emotions as I pondered in my heart all that had just occurred.

# Chapter One

## REFLECTION

*When burdened with an intense desire to have another child, but deeply discouraged by a lack of results, I decided to ask God directly for intervention through the intercession of St. Thérèse of Lisieux. I prayed a novena with great faith that Jesus could indeed answer my cry for help and with a firm conviction that with Him all things are possible. When given confirmation that my prayers were heard, I became a person who knows without a doubt the power of prayer. I learned to confidently ask our good and merciful God for what my heart specifically yearns and to wait with great expectation for His response.*

**Questions**

1. How have you dealt with discouragement when a dream of yours didn't seem to be working out?
2. Is there a weighty burden that you are carrying right now that you know you can't alleviate on your own?
3. Have you considered asking God for what you need or desire with confident hope that He will hear and answer your prayers? What method of prayer could you use?
4. Can you recall a time when you prayed and were overwhelmed by the Lord's generous and loving response? What did that answer to prayer look like?

**Prayer Experience**

*Get in a comfortable prayer posture, settle in, and pray through each section. Begin and end the prayer in a way that you prefer and are familiar with. (Example: In the name of the Father, and of the Son, and of the Holy Spirit. Amen.) Let's be people of great faith who ask the Lord with our whole selves for what our hearts desperately long for . . . and wait with great expectation for what He will do!*

- **Praise** God for His goodness and for listening to the cries of His beloved children.
- **Ask** the Holy Spirit to come and be with you as you think about a specific situation in which you are in need of something you can't attain on your own.
- When you are ready, boldly and respectfully **ask** Jesus for what you desire with great confidence that He will hear and answer your prayers.
- **Thank** the Lord ahead of time for the way He'll respond, trusting that His answers and plans are good.
- **Be expectant and ready to receive** what God has for you! Remember: with God, nothing is impossible!

CHAPTER 2

# Triple Blessing

*"May it be done to me according to your word."*

—Lk 1:38

A COUPLE weeks after the roses had appeared, I began showing signs of being pregnant: bouts of morning sickness, headaches, and extreme tiredness. I truly believed I was with child, but I cautiously waited for medical confirmation. On the next routine visit, our doctor verified that I was indeed pregnant. My husband and I were thrilled! We decided not to tell people right away, though, until we were a little further into the pregnancy.

At six weeks along, we found ourselves in the doctor's office again. This appointment was for our first ultrasound, and Dave and Johnny were with me. We were eager to see how things were going. After a long wait, the fertility specialist finally made his way into our sterile little cubicle of a room. As he entered, he extended a hand to greet us and even said a few playful words to my toddler as he bounced around the room. After a few more pleasantries, the doctor confidently reconfirmed that we were really pregnant and that my progesterone levels were rising at a rapid rate. He then told me that he was going to administer an internal ultrasound to hear the baby's heartbeat and check and see how things were going. I climbed on the examining table and looked excitedly at Dave and Johnny in anticipation of hearing more about our expanding family. The doctor began the exam with his ultrasound instrument while looking intently at the computer screen in front of him. He did this for a couple minutes in silence while we eagerly waited to hear some news.

In a moment that has been etched forever in my brain, the doctor looked directly into my eyes and gently placed a hand on my foot. He then said quietly, "There's a lot going on in here." He proceeded to tell us that there was not one, not two, but *three* babies growing inside me at once.

I'm not quite sure of the details in the tornado of language he uttered next, but certain words and phrases jumped out at me: "triplets" . . . "the possibility of bed rest" . . . "trying to make it to twenty-eight or thirty-two weeks" . . . "complications" . . . "the probability of premature birth and birth defects" . . . "having a procedure called a selective reduction". . . .

Suddenly I snapped out of it. I happened to know that a "selective reduction" is doctor terminology for an abortive procedure that takes the life of one or two babies inside the mother to give a better chance for the other one(s) to live.

This was the first option the doctor suggested to me after dropping the news that I was carrying triplets.

I didn't even need a minute to think about my answer. There was absolutely no way I was going to take the life of one or two of these children for whom I prayed so hard. There was *no way* I could destroy these utter gifts that God had so graciously given to me. I spoke up without hesitation and authoritatively said, "*No*! We are *not* going to have a selective reduction. I'm going to have these babies!"

The doctor turned and said, "Are you okay?"

I thought he was speaking to me, but apparently, he was more concerned with my husband, Dave. I looked over at him, and he was as white as a ghost. He told me later that his whole torso had broken out in a rash. He was truly in shock and instantly thought he might vomit everywhere as soon as the words *three babies* spilled out of the doctor's mouth.

Dave was struck mute as we looked at each other in utter disbelief. The doctor continued his exam and said that he heard three healthy heartbeats. We were informed that at this stage of pregnancy, babies grow quickly and are about the size of raspberries. Their bodies are continuing to develop as their tiny arms, fingers, legs, and toes take shape and their brains, hearts, and other organs continue to grow. We went through the rest of the visit trying to take it all in.

The drive home is when I lost it. The emotional composure I had exhibited during most of the doctor's visit was now completely gone. The reality of being pregnant with triplets and how our lives were about to drastically change descended on me with an oppressive force. In all honesty, fear was my initial reaction. I'm a small woman with a tiny frame. *How could someone 5'4" and 110 pounds carry triplets to term? I couldn't even carry one baby to term. Johnny was born a month ahead of schedule, and he was just a singleton! And where were we going to house these unexpected extra children? How could I feed three babies at once? What about a car that could hold four car seats?* The questions were rolling through my head at a dizzying pace. Soon enough, my anxiety and feelings of being totally overwhelmed splashed out in the form of tears. Dave kept quiet on the drive home.

As we got closer to our house, I felt an urge to tell my parents the news in person. I asked my husband to drive us the extra thirty minutes to their home, and he agreed. I felt like I needed to tell someone else and have their support right from the start. I called my mom and asked if we could stop over for a minute. She said, "Sure."

As we stood in the driveway of my parents' tan brick house, I paused for a moment and drew comfort from this place where I'd spent my most formative years. I grew up in this suburban home. I spent lazy summer afternoons kicking the soccer ball against the wall of this house. I wished on a star that I would marry an amazing man right on the lawn outside of this home. I had many slumber parties there with my friends, played video games with my sisters, had many family dinners and parties both inside and out, made home movies and obstacle courses on the driveway, played and fought with my siblings here, and created poetry in this house. Just being there gave me some comfort and reminded me of simpler times and happy memories.

As I mused over these fond recollections, my small child tugged on my pant leg, and my dreamlike bubble burst right there on the driveway and snapped me back to the present moment. The new certainty of being pregnant with triplets sunk deeper into my being as I made my way toward the house. I walked right through the front door without even so much as a knock, with my husband and son following close behind. I saw my parents and plopped down at the kitchen table.

My mom and dad knew that we had a doctor's appointment that day and naturally asked us how it went. I could barely muster up the courage to even say the words, but I somehow managed to announce, "Mom, Dad . . . we're having . . . triplets!"

My mom instantly got the biggest smile on her face and was so excited she could barely contain herself. Her reply caught me completely off guard, as I was expecting more of a tempered response.

*How can she be so excited?* I thought to myself. *Doesn't she know the risks involved in this type of pregnancy? Isn't she worried for my health and the health of these babies? How can she be thrilled when I am so afraid?*

* * *

I spent the next several weeks and months getting ready. Once I got past the 'I can't believe this is happening' phase, I moved into the full-blown 'preparation' phase. If this was about to become my reality, I wanted to be prepared. I was a competitive swimmer growing up, and my mindset changed from wallowing in fear and being overwhelmed by the news to training for the biggest race of my life. I began to see this as an Ironwoman Competition, and I went all in. I stopped everything else in my life to prepare for it. I quit my graduate classes in religious studies in the middle of the semester so I could focus on getting ready full time. I knew there was no way I could continue working toward a master's degree once the triplets were born anyway, so I quit. I also discontinued my volunteer work with the youth group because I needed adequate time to prepare for this monumental change in my life. I was letting go of a few things to make room for triple the people in my life.

With the extra time on my hands and a whole new mindset, I went into serious planning mode. I'm the type of person that likes to research, get all my ducks in a row, map out a strategy, and then be flexible with executing the plan. One of the first things I did was send out a group email to close family and friends to share the news and garner support.

---

**EMAIL**

## Baby, Baby, Baby

***March 13, 2007***

Hello, friends and family. A few of you know this already, but we wanted to let all of you know that Dave and I are finally pregnant . . . with triplets!

That's right—three little heartbeats, three little bodies, three little angels sent from above! We all must have prayed pretty hard to get this kind of outcome. We are at eight weeks right now, and we just had an ultrasound today. All is going well with the babies thus far.

Dave and I have run the gamut of emotions already, since we found out we were having three babies at just six weeks along. We've felt overwhelmed, anxious, downright afraid, and just recently excited. So many thoughts, questions, fears, and things to prepare have gone through our minds, as you might imagine.

This pregnancy is considered very high-risk since the babies will inevitably be born prematurely (probably between twenty-eight and thirty-two weeks). I will most likely be on bed rest for a couple months, and we will surely be in the hospital a while once the babies are born and are being taken care of in the NICU. Despite the risks, we've heard of at least five other people living in our area that have had triplets successfully and are more than willing to meet with us, give us advice, etc. It's nice to know that we are not alone in this, and that people have done this before. . . .

Right now we are in need of extra prayers (for courage, strength, peace of mind, and health for myself, Dave, and all three babies), extra things (cribs, highchairs, changing tables, rockers, bouncy seats, etc.), and extra help (while I'm on bed rest to keep me sane and to help take care of Johnny, and once the babies are born with probably just about anything).

Besides all the difficulties this journey brings, we have pondered its gifts as well. Dave and I always wanted to have four children in our family; I'll get to eat for four now; and our house will soon be bursting with LIFE!

If nothing else, PLEASE pray for us. The love of family and friends surrounding us and supporting us will surely see us through. God knows that we CANNOT do this alone.

Thank you and we love you,
Jules, Dave, Johnny, baby 1, baby 2, baby 3

P.S. We'll keep you updated as things progress.

---

Once the news got out and started spreading, it was amazing how people, organizations, and other resources about having multiples suddenly presented themselves to us: "So-and-so has triplets and she'd be glad to answer any of your questions"; "There's a multiples group in town that can give you information and provide support during the pregnancy and afterward"; etc. Who knew there was this underground group of moms with twins, triplets, and quadruplets, and resources at the ready to support others who found themselves in similar circumstances?

One of the first things I wanted to figure out was how to deal with the quandary of where these babies were going to sleep once they arrived. We are blessed to have a house big enough to fit everyone, but we had to reimagine our spaces and shuffle some things around. We figured we could use our smallest bedroom for our office area and transform our larger 'bonus room' over the garage for the triplets so they could all be together, at least while they were babies.

This was the fun part for me: imagining three cribs lined up with charmingly sweet bedding and envisioning three cute little sleeping babies in them. I really enjoyed figuring out paint colors and deciding where the furniture would go. Of course, we already had one crib, but I'd have to figure out how to scrounge up two more. I realized that I'd have to find two more of everything—two more highchairs, two more baby bathtubs, twice as many bottles, and double the number of toys and clothes than I already had. I'd also need more car seats, for sure.

That brought me to my next item of business: finding a vehicle that could transport all of us around town. The car we had at the time couldn't accommodate three baby car seats, a toddler car seat, and two adults. I imagined the Yost bus coming down the street and everyone recognizing our family lugging around our extra-large crew. We'd be the talk of the town for sure! We wanted something practical, yet not bus-like.

It was quite humorous going to car dealerships and explaining the situation. We even brought Johnny's car seat along as a prop as we explained that we would need enough space for three more baby seats. Once we got past the looks of sheer disbelief, the car salesmen seemed genuinely more than happy to help us find something suitable.

We settled on a giant used SUV. It was like nothing I'd driven before—a big tan beast of a vehicle fully capable of hauling a mother-load of children and all the things that accompanied them. It wasn't the most fuel-efficient machine, but it would do the job. I couldn't imagine going for long trips with that many infants anyway. It would get me to the babies' doctors' appointments, grandparents' homes, and the grocery store just fine without too much damage to the environment.

We sold our car, signed the documents, and purchased the SUV. The big tan beast was now ours. When we first pulled that extra-large automobile into our relatively small driveway, it took up three-quarters of the space and wouldn't fit into our already cramped garage. This was a signal to the neighbors that something new was on the horizon for the Yost family. Once we parked, I looked in the rearview mirror and saw little Johnny alone in the back of that massive vehicle that would soon be filled with three other tiny people. This was becoming more real . . . and I was getting more and more excited!

As I continued to research, plan, and prepare, I wanted to make sure I covered all my bases. In addition to considering the practical logistics, I wanted to make sure I was prepared spiritually and emotionally for the arduous journey ahead. I began looking for a spiritual guide to help me navigate this experience and give me support and encouragement when needed. I discovered that our church had a pastoral counselor on staff whose name was Rosie—another rose God sent my way.

I called the parish office and arranged an appointment to meet with Rosie to see if she would be a good fit for my personality and current needs. Rosie was an older woman with gray hair, a solid build, and a grandmotherly presence. She kindly shook my hand and welcomed me with a warm smile. Her small, carpeted office was simple yet comfortable. There was a wall of books and some simple pictures and other décor that made me feel like I was entering her living room. She told me that she was glad I was there and invited me to share what brought me to see her.

As I began to divulge the details of my situation, Rosie listened intently and allowed me to talk openly and without judgment about my story, my struggles, my hopes, and my fears. I didn't think I'd get so emotional, but I actually teared up a couple times in front of this relative stranger as I poured everything out to her. Rosie offered me tissues as she continued to listen to my concerns. It was cathartic just to talk about my situation out loud with an unbiased and compassionate listener—especially after a rough night of bad dreams and a morning filled with sickness and nausea.

Rosie was a rock and knew just what to say to offer me comfort and hope. She actually had a niece who was built similarly to me who recently had quadruplets! She told me that her niece's babies were born a little bit early but came out just fine. They were all happy and healthy ten-year-olds now. This story gave me hope that what I was attempting to do was possible. Also, for her to have intimate knowledge of this type of pregnancy was incredibly reassuring.

Rosie then prayed with me, offered to be with me whenever needed on this journey, and gave me some advice that I immediately took to heart. Knowing I would be likely to go on bed rest before forty weeks' gestation (which is considered full-term), she told me to go into this time knowing it is a marathon, not a sprint, and to consider this pregnancy as a retreat: journaling, praying, and letting God lead me every step of the way, one day at a time. Finally, she said, "Julie . . . you were chosen for this," as if this was *the* most special thing I would ever be called upon to do. Those words reverberated through my body, and I left there feeling inspired, full of purpose, and more ready to face the challenges ahead.

After this special visit, I began a prayer journal and started to write my thoughts and prayers in it regularly.

---

*Journal Entry*
*March 22, 2007*
*Week 9*

*Thank you for Rosie, Lord, and for the gift of her wisdom and her prayers. Thank you also for the space you created to allow me to cry openly . . . tears of fear, tears of joy, and tears of being in awe of You in the midst of it all. I'm beginning to see all of this as a gift, as part of Your plan and to teach me great things. Help me to be open to Your will. Prepare my mind, my heart, and my body for this great sacrifice.*

*Strengthen me, love me, give me the grace I need to rise up to this challenge. This is my cross right now. Help me to carry it with love, support, and faith, knowing that You only give good things to Your children. I loved when Rosie said, "These babies have touched so many lives already." Indeed, they have. They are special human beings . . . already. You only create wonderfully good things. I thank You for honoring me in such a special way. Help me to constantly, like Your mother, Mary, say "yes!"*

*Please bless Dave, too, and my little sweetie John. Give them strength and courage, too, and fill them with Your peaceful and lifegiving spirit.*

*I love You. Stay with me. Keep me in the palm of Your hand. Guide me.*

*Your child,*
*Jules*

---

At thirteen weeks along, things were going relatively well. We had another ultrasound at the doctor's office and were told that all three babies had strong heartbeats, were growing at a healthy and steady rate, and were moving around like crazy inside me! It was truly miraculous to see all the things going on in my uterus simultaneously on the screen. We got to keep the pictures from the ultrasound, and one of the babies was looking straight at us with his or her hand in the air as if waving to us. We could see all five fingers, too!

During this first trimester of my pregnancy, my belly popped out like a balloon, and I looked like I was further along in the pregnancy than I actually was. I was getting pretty sick in the mornings, too: severe bouts of nausea, vomiting, headaches, and extreme tiredness. Who knew that growing three babies at once could be so exhausting? My hormones were on overdrive as well, and I had some really difficult days when I couldn't muster the strength to get out of bed because of the misery I felt until around 4:00 p.m. or so. But I'd also have good days when I had a lot more energy and could handle a bit more. Those awful days helped me appreciate the good days so much more.

When I wasn't feeling well, it was really hard to play with and take care of Johnny, who was at such a sweet and needy stage of life. I felt extremely blessed, though, to have a wonderful husband and family members who lived close by and were willing to help when times got rough.

During this time, Dave brought me saltine crackers and juice every morning to help curb the early day sickness, and he helped take care of Johnny before he went to work. In this phase in his life, our little John man would get up around 5:00 a.m., ready to take on the world. Dave would lug his tired body downstairs with Johnny, feed him some oatmeal and milk, and put on a cartoon while he snoozed next to him on the couch. I believe the record was four episodes of a cartoon, back-to-back-to-back-to-back. Since I was normally a stickler about screen time with our son, I could only imagine Johnny feeling like he was in heaven being able to watch so much TV.

Our two-year-old got so accustomed to this new routine that one day he decided *not* to wake up Mommy and Daddy, to toddle down the stairs and proceed to turn on the television all by himself and watch a show, solo. We discovered him downstairs later that morning, looking like a teenager just chillin' in front of the screen. I found out later that he was unknowingly watching a grown-up police show that scared him a little. I guess none of us went unscathed during this crazy time when rules were bent and things began to shift just so we could function.

In addition to my husband, I had a dedicated host of people that would show up to help during these early days of my triplet experience. My sisters took turns taking care of Johnny when I couldn't even get up or move around, my mom came over a couple times a week to watch Johnny, cook, and help clean our house, and even my aunts and in-laws took turns taking care of Johnny and offered to grocery shop or clean while I was feeling ill and Dave was at work.

---

*Journal Entry*
*April 21, 2007*
*Week 14*

*I am overwhelmed with love and support. I sometimes hate that I need so much help and feel a little like I can't do anything, but I know I can't do it alone. I know I'll need even more help here as time goes on.*

*Thank You, Lord, for my support network. They are gifts from You. Help me to rest, prepare, and take care of myself and the babies at this time. Continue to give me strength and courage to overcome all the struggles ahead, and help the babies continue to be safe and healthy. Bless my body, too. Help me to be strong enough to do whatever it takes to give these babies a good life outside the womb. Like Rosie said, these babies have touched lives already, and they've brought our family together. I am thankful they're inside of me.*

*I love you,*
*Jules*

---

As I entered into the second trimester of my pregnancy, I found out I was carrying one boy and two girls. We wanted to be surprised by the gender of our first child, but since there were three babies coming at once this time, we thought it would be best to know in advance so we could be better prepared. We now had three names to pick out instead of just one, and knowing their genders and how many names of each were needed was something concrete we could consider at this point.

Just knowing the sexes of the babies made everything so much more real! I could now envision the triplet bedroom better with two cribs for girls and one for a boy. I could also picture three highchairs with my two daughters and son in them as well as figuring out clothing options and other things. I pictured Johnny hanging out with his little brother and the two girls being the best of friends. What fun to just sit and imagine the future!

Knowing the babies' genders also helped with registering items at our local baby superstore, especially since my family decided it would be a good idea to have a baby shower. At around eighteen weeks' gestation, my family planned a gift-giving party to help me collect the necessary baby supplies. The shower took place at my house, with my family and a few close friends in attendance. The decorations were hung, the treats were made, and the women I loved were invited. This was the next big step in this whole ordeal becoming even more real.

During the shower, my dearest friends and family members couldn't help but comment on how big my belly was already. I actually looked like I could deliver at any moment even though I was only a little over four months along. We enjoyed sharing stories, people offered their help and support once the babies arrived, and we chatted about how unbelievable this all was.

During the gift portion of the party, I accumulated highchairs, bouncy seats, cribs, clothes, feeding items, strollers, and more. Our home began to look like a Babies R Us warehouse! All of these gifts, however, made me realize the game-changing magnitude of the situation and anticipate all the life—the craziness, messiness, laughter, tears, and joy—that was about to enter it. I could just imagine attempting to feed them all at once, the sound of all the little feet running through the house when they grew to be toddlers, the funny antics they would pull as a triplet team, and just how much fuller my world was about to become.

Little did I know that I'd only be home for about a week longer. . . .

# *Chapter Two*

## REFLECTION

*When hearing the shocking news that my prayers to have another baby were answered by being pregnant with triplets, I had a life-altering choice to make. I had to decide whether to say "yes" or "no" to the gifts of life inside of me and to agree or not to this new plan without fully understanding it or knowing exactly what it would entail. By God's grace, I had the faith to trust that God knew what He was doing and the courage to surrender my own vision of how my family would unfold. In being obedient and aligning myself with God's will and Church teachings, God immediately stepped in and began to perfectly give me everything that was needed for this step of the journey. God is just waiting for our trust-filled "yes" to His good and perfect ways and for our permission to let Him take over. He will provide!*

**Questions**

1. Have you experienced a moment when you had to make a countercultural decision that aligned with your faith? If yes, what was that experience like for you?
2. Think about an instance when you were asked to let go of your own desires out of love for another or for the sake of God's will. Were you able to do it or not? How did that response make you feel?

3. How has God provided for you during times when you've let go of your own agenda and trusted in His design for your life?

**Prayer Experience**

*Let's be people of great faith who humbly and obediently submit our plans to the One who knows us and loves us the best. When the Lord asks something of us, let us, like Mother Mary, say, "Yes, Lord, may it be done to me according to your word."*

- **Praise** God for His divine and beautiful plans for your life.
- **Ask** Jesus to come close and speak to you about what He desires for you right now and where He wants you to let go of your own plan in order to embrace His even better one.
- In an act of total trust and surrender, **ask** God for the courage and strength to say "yes" to what He is asking of you.
- When you're ready, **declare** out loud with all of your heart, "Do whatever You think is best, Lord. May it be done to me according to Your beautiful design."
- **Thank** God in advance for the ways He'll supply everything you need and be ready to receive the blessings and provision God has for you as you align your will with His plan!

CHAPTER 3

# My Side of the Curtain

*"Behold, I stand at the door and knock. If anyone hears my voice and opens the door, [then] I will enter his house and dine with him, and he with me."*

—Rv 3:20

MY CONTRACTIONS began at nineteen weeks' gestation, which is just barely into the second trimester of pregnancy. They were happening pretty frequently—as many as twelve in an hour and sometimes as often as every three minutes! I also started to get a cramping feeling in my uterus, and I hoped that nothing was seriously wrong. My husband and I began to get a little worried and thought it best to go to the hospital and get things checked out by our doctors who specialized in pregnancies involving multiples.

After the initial hospital intake procedures, I was put in a glorious half-room with a curtain down the middle that separated me from my pregnant teenage roommate. It was pretty awkward at times as we'd each have to get some invasive procedures done just a couple feet away from each other. Though the drapery gave the pretense of privacy, every word could be heard from visitors, phone conversations, and the nurses and doctors in the room. Talk about confidentiality! After just a little while in that room, I found out that the young lady in the bed next to me got pregnant by her boyfriend at the time. I knew this because there would be lengthy phone calls in which she'd be yelling at her 'baby daddy' for various reasons. I wasn't sure how long I could deal with this situation, since I was worried about my own medical issues and was used to having some semblance of privacy and quietness. I prayed that I'd be back in my own home in no time.

My visit to the hospital was fraught with complications. To slow down the contractions, the doctors gave me a drug called Brethine, which is a smooth muscle relaxer. I experienced some pretty serious negative reactions to this medication, however. Soon after it was given, my entire body began to shake, I came right to the edge of blacking out, and my heart started racing. Because of these adverse effects, the doctors decided to take me off the Brethine and check out my heart with an EKG. It turned out that my heart was beating an extra time (a condition known as premature ventricular contractions, or PVCs) even after stopping the drug, so an echocardiogram was also ordered to make sure my heart was okay.

As I waited for the heart ultrasound to be administered, the contractions began to slow down on their own and Dave and I thought we'd be going home soon if the echo turned out okay. No such luck. The contractions started coming again at a regular rate. The doctors checked my cervix, but luckily everything was still closed, and the babies were doing fine as well.

We waited for what seemed like an inordinate amount of time for this heart test to be completed. To pass the time, Dave and I decided to figure out ways to find amusement on my side of the curtain. My husband managed to score some playing cards from the gift shop and some serious gin rummy battles ensued at my bedside. At other times, we would just sit and talk and crack up about the whole situation. It almost felt like we were on a date—without our toddler, and minus the exotic location.

Dave has always had quite a way with words, and he knows how to get me giggling in any situation, even this one. My abdomen was strapped to a tocodynamometer (a device that measures the frequency and duration of contractions), and Dave got me chuckling so hard that the meter went crazy from my belly violently shaking with laughter. The nurses mistook the information showing up on their end of the computer screen as me having an onslaught of contractions. They rushed in to see what was wrong, only to find out I was just laughing really hard.

Finally, after several hours had passed, the technician doing the heart ultrasound came by to see me. I found out later that she made a special trip to the hospital on her day off just to make sure that the "lady with the triplets" was doing okay. As she methodically scoured every angle of my heart with her mechanical wand and viewed the live imaging on the screen, she said that she didn't see anything initially jumping out to her that was concerning. She did, however, need to get the official results from the cardiologist later on.

Since it was late in the evening and I wouldn't get the official results until the morning, I would have to stay overnight, possibly for a couple days. We decided it would be best for Dave to go back home so he could relieve my mom of babysitting duty. I was left to myself, my new teenage best friend, and my thoughts.

It turned out that I couldn't sleep very well while pregnant on an uncomfortable mattress, next to a person I barely knew, and in unfamiliar surroundings. I couldn't go anywhere, and various nurses stopped by periodically to check on us throughout the night. With all the new sounds and inconvenient disturbances, who could sleep well in those conditions? Not me, that's for sure!

I think I did manage to get a few hours of periodic shut-eye that night. Before I knew it, though, it was morning, the doctors were starting to make rounds, and my breakfast would soon be delivered. Despite the rough night, I thought, *That's at least kind of cool . . . not to have to make breakfast AND have it delivered right to my bed. Not a bad start to a Saturday morning!* Though the eggs, sausage, fruit cup, and orange juice weren't of supreme quality, it gave me a fun grade school-like flashback to eating cafeteria food on a tray.

Dave came back to visit in the morning soon after that, just in time for one of my doctors, Dr. P, to check in with us. This doctor was tall and slender and had the best bedside manner. He sat right in the chair next to me and talked with me in a compassionate and gentle way, making me feel comfortable and at ease. He was intelligent and experienced, but he also found a way to describe things in a simple manner that we nonmedical people could understand. I felt like I was in the best of care, and that put me at ease.

Dr. P confirmed that everything they saw on the ultrasound was indeed okay. And since my heart was now deemed in good shape, he put me on another medication to try and slow down or stop my continual contractions. He prescribed a drug called Procardia, a blood pressure medicine that also happens to work to relax uterine contractions and postpone preterm labor.

About thirty minutes later, a new round of negative reactions ensued. My whole body started shaking, my nose started bleeding, and when I got up to use the restroom, all the blood rushed to my feet and they turned bright red. Feelings of worry crept back in.

Right in the middle of these anxious thoughts and weird side effects, a chaplain knocked on my door and came in, asked if I was Mrs. Yost, and wanted to know if I'd like to receive Holy Communion. I said yes, and he began with some simple yet beautiful prayers filled with consolation and hope. Then he gave me the Eucharist and said a few more encouraging words to me. A sense of peace began to swell in my heart and settled in as this holy man concluded his short visit and left my room. My negative side effects of the new drug began diminishing, too. I didn't realize until later how stunningly profound that moment was.

After resting quietly for a while in my room, Dr. P returned and confirmed what my body had already begun to know: the new drug was now working well to minimize my contractions. He reiterated that my heart was doing fine, too. This was all good news! He even said that I'd probably be able to go home the next day. He instructed me to keep taking the medicine regularly at home and ordered me to go on pretty strict bed rest until the babies were born. That was a hopeful report as far as I was concerned, because now I could at least be in the comfort of my own home with my family and friends around me.

After the doctor's visit, Dave left the hospital to go to work. I took a short nap and was surprised to wake up to some very special people who came to visit. My sister, Katie, made the trip out with my son, Johnny, and they instantly brightened up my day. There's nothing like a sweet little two-year-old to make everything alright and put things in perspective. My sister brought in some board books that I read to my little boy, and then he played with my hospital bed by pushing the buttons to make it go up and down. He even climbed up and slid down the "hill" of the bed when the top was raised up high. It was so nice to see my son again, especially knowing that I'd soon be back home with him full-time.

Even though I'd have to spend the next few months pretty much just lying around as the babies continued to grow and develop in my womb, I would at least still be in Johnny's presence on a regular basis as his mom. I missed our special times together, especially our snack times and bedtime chats. I was determined to find a way to make the at-home bed rest situation work. Anything was better than being in the hospital cooped up in a cramped and sterile environment away from my family. The next day I went home.

---

*Journal Entry*
*May 27, 2007*
*Week 19*

*It was really hard being in that one room for three days. I just couldn't sleep. The bed was uncomfortable, I was sharing a room with another pregnant lady, and there were nurses and doctors and noises at all times, even throughout the night. Not to mention the gnats...*

*But I must talk about the joys and graces of being confined to one little space for three days. One night when I couldn't sleep, I decided to reflect on my day by using the Ignatian Examen method. One part of it was to go through your day in detail and think about all that you were grateful for. There were many things. . . .*

*There was a special grace I didn't totally realize the significance of until I started reflecting on it. A priest had stopped in briefly because I had written on a form about a month or so ago that I was Catholic. I had totally forgotten that it was a Saturday afternoon—and Pentecost weekend, of all weekends. He asked me if I was Mrs. Yost and if I'd like to receive Holy Communion, and I said, "Yes." He said some prayers of comfort which brought tears to my eyes, and then he left.*

*What I realize now is that Jesus Christ Himself came to my door and called me by name. Jesus is still coming to visit the sick today, offering peace and healing. What I couldn't get over while reflecting was that Jesus found me! He came to me like He always does when I need Him the most. I just had to accept or deny if I wanted Him to be there. There I was, "locked up," if you will—not seeing even so much as the hallway outside my door for two days—and Jesus came to ME! I felt such an overwhelming sense of peace and love that I believe I fell asleep . . . even if just for an hour!*

*Thank you for being with me, God. Continue to bless this journey and everyone on it with me. Give us strength and courage to bring forth these three new lives inside of me.*

*—Mrs. Yost*

---

# Chapter Three

## REFLECTION

*When faced with a three-day hospitalization for early contractions, I experienced some inconveniences and a few health scares. I was blessed to have family support at home and to be in the company of my loving husband and great doctors and nurses in the hospital. The most amazing thing, though, was how Jesus unexpectedly showed up in my hospital room in the form of the Eucharist to be with me and offer sustenance and hope in my time of need. I just had to open the door, recognize His presence, and let Him in to receive the merciful and generous gift of Himself that He was offering. How blessed are we to have a God who sees us, loves us, and provides for us in personal and intimate ways, and wants so desperately to be close to us in both the joyful and stressful moments of our lives!*

**Questions**

1. Think of a time when you've been through a troubling situation. Did you invite anyone in to help shoulder that burden? Was that easy or difficult for you to do?
2. How can having a positive attitude and a spirit of gratitude help during times of trial?
3. What graces or joys have you experienced in the midst of a challenging season?

4. Can you recall a moment when the Lord broke into your distress at exactly the right time and came to the door of your heart offering peace or healing? If so, what was that like and were you able to let Him in and receive His love for you?

**Prayer Experience**

*Let's be people of great faith who are willing to give God permission to enter our beautiful and messy situations. May we be able to recognize and receive the love and provision He has for us.*

- **Praise** God for never abandoning His people and for always wanting to be near to us.
- **Imagine** Jesus is standing at the door of your heart knocking right now, just waiting to be let in. With confident trust in our loving God, **invite** Jesus into your heart right now. Feel His presence as close as your breath.
- **Ask** the Lord to come into a difficult or challenging area of your life. Allow Him to sit with you in it like a dear friend. Be open to what He wants to say and do in this place.
- **Be still** and let Jesus love you. Be ready to receive whatever healing, peace, and encouragement He has for you today!
- Joyfully **thank God** for His presence with you and for the grace and love He's pouring out.

CHAPTER 4

# Hotel Good Sam

*"No one has greater love than this, to lay down one's life for one's friends."*

—Jn 15:13

AT THE end of my nineteenth week of pregnancy, I was readmitted to the hospital . . . this time to stay. My cervix had started to thin and I was contracting regularly, so the doctors wanted to keep me close for observation and manage my high-risk pregnancy from there for the best possible outcome. I shared a room with another woman again as the doctors assessed my situation. When they determined that I would need to stay in the hospital for the duration of the pregnancy on strict bed rest, I was moved to my own small, private room. This was a tough pill to swallow. *Strict bed rest? In the hospital? What does that even mean?* I wondered. But this was a sacrifice I was willingly ready to accept as I'd heard before that this could be a possibility in situations like mine. Little did I know what I was really signing up for and about to endure.

My new room had bland, white walls that enhanced its cold, sterile motif. My bed was perpendicular to the right wall and had a button to raise and lower the top half. It was also equipped with a call button to reach out to a nurse in case of an emergency. Straight across from my bed was a small bathroom with a toilet, sink, and minuscule shower with a seat in it and railings to hold on to for extra support. There were also a few moveable tray tables in my room, a TV, a dry erase board on the wall, monitors, and a stiff, fold out chair that a visitor could sit on (or sleep on if necessary). My *favorite* feature was the window to the right of my bed. Eager to see what my view would be for the next few months as I got situated, I opened the blinds to find that it looked out at a lovely scene . . . a brick wall just inches away from the glass! I decided to keep the blinds shut.

Determined not to let the barren landscape of my room get me down, I decided to decorate a bit to make it a bit cheerier and homier. Just like in college, I decided to put a splattering of inspirational quotes and a couple large posters on the walls. One picture was of three cute babies sitting in metal washtubs taking a bath. It made me smile and gave me a friendly reminder to stay put. I also constructed a bright, handmade countdown calendar that I used to mark off the days as they went by. I highlighted the goal dates on the calendar that we hoped to reach in the pregnancy: twenty-eight weeks, then thirty-two weeks, then thirty-five weeks. These three colorful calendar sheets were set for June, July, and August and hung on the wall. It was May 28 when I began my stay at "Hotel Good Sam" (as the other women staying on my floor with high-risk pregnancies fondly referred to it). I had a long way to go! My due date was at the end of October.

As I settled into this new space, I slowly began to adjust to the rhythms and routines of hospital life. Who knew I'd ever take up residency at a hospital . . . and at thirty years of age! My first assignment was to don a beautifully designed gown that was teal in color and had a small, patterned print. It fell slightly below the knee and tied in two places with strings across my back. The nurse handed it to me as if to say, "Prisoner #32, here are your clothes for the duration of your time here. Get used to it. You won't need to worry about wardrobe choices anymore. I hope you like both its lack of comfort and style."

My next, and most important, order of business was to lie flat on my back or on my side—*all* day and *all* night . . . *every . . . single . . . day*. Standing, walking, or sitting upright for too long would bring on more contractions and cause the babies to be delivered way too early. My only reprieve from this strict rule was when I ate, went to the restroom, or took a quick shower. When my meals arrived, I had the joy of pushing the button to raise my bed just long enough so I could pull my tray of food over, scarf down the hospital grub, and then lower back down afterward. The staff recommended that I didn't shower every day because that was just too much standing and would put unnecessary pressure on my uterus. I really didn't work up a sweat lying around all day anyway and didn't have anyone to impress. Once in the shower, I could wash up for just a minute or two and then head back to my horizontal state. I decided to scrap the idea of trying to look halfway decent early on, as well. As long as I brushed my hair and teeth and put on a little deodorant, I was set. No need for make-up, jewelry, or anything else. It was kind of freeing in a weird sort of way.

Next was the daily hospital routine. I found out quickly that you can't get more than four hours of sleep at a time even if you try, due to nurses and doctors going on rounds and doing checks 24/7. I suppose it was necessary for someone to roll her cart in my room at 2:00 a.m. to make sure I still had a pulse, take my temperature, and give me more meds. So much for getting a solid seven or eight hours of shut-eye! This was just part of the deal, though, and I took to napping throughout the day as needed.

One of my favorite, and sometimes only, amusements of my day-to-day life was in the morning when I reviewed the paper menu listing the items available for each meal of the day. This was *the* one thing I had control over during this whole ordeal, so I didn't take my meal choices lightly. It was a delightfully fun process, actually, to peruse the menu with great deliberation and mark down my selections for the meals that day. *Am I feeling like chicken or a burger today? Should I go with the salad or mixed veggies? Did I want an ice cream cup or a Jell-O square for dessert?* Since I didn't have much to do in the hospital, the simple things began to matter so much more, and I began to find joy in them.

My consistent company and main source of human interaction became the people employed at the hospital: the doctors and nurses, the cafeteria workers, the maintenance and cleaning crew, etc. I realized they would be my new community for a while—my new neighbors so to speak—so I became friendly with the people I saw on a daily basis. There was Rosetta (yet another rose God sent my way), who came in every weekday to tidy up my room. We'd chat for a few minutes if I was awake, and we began to learn about each other's lives. It was so nice to see her familiar, friendly face regularly as she cleaned my room. We became fast friends, and it was a highlight of my day when she'd pop in for a while. Then there was Carol, one of the lovely angels who brought my food up from the kitchen directly to my room. We would talk a bit every time she brought in a new meal. Sometimes she would even sneak in an extra treat for me if she knew there was something I especially liked. She knew I was eating for four.

There were also rotating nurses and doctors who I came to know and grew fond of. I loved the ones who would take the time to sit with me for a moment or two and genuinely ask about my life and see how I was *really* doing. It reaffirmed for me that there really are amazing people anywhere you go, and that a supportive community is essential for living well and getting through tough times.

I also enjoyed spending time and being in contact with people I knew on a deeper level. Besides the everyday cast of characters who would enter my world and interact with me daily, other friends, family members, and former co-workers would sporadically make the trip out to see me, send emails, or call. This was right at the dawn of the internet when flip phones and emails were a big deal, so calls, emails, and in-person visits were the best forms of communication at the time. These ongoing visits and messages from family members and friends gave me an overwhelming sense of support and strength that I needed to push through. Some visits early on stand out in my memory.

My Aunt Judy came to see me once during one of my first days on strict hospital bed rest. She came to my door one afternoon bearing gifts. She entered my room with a smile and brought me a small off-white and gold stuffed angel ornament, which she immediately attached to my IV pole. She also brought in some fresh goodies from her garden that I could munch on. I remember trying to be polite during her visit and engage in conversation with her, but I was really tired and not feeling so well that day. She sensed this after a few moments and told me that it was okay if I closed my eyes and rested. She said she would just sit in the chair and pray for me if that was okay. I agreed wholeheartedly, as I'd never been given such a kind and thoughtful offer before. I was so thankful she was there and gave me permission to rest and not have to entertain her.

As I closed my eyes, I remember feeling so at peace knowing someone was in my room praying for me while I rested. When I woke up about an hour later, she was still sitting there quietly praying a Rosary for me. My aunt gave me more in that silence than she would ever know. What a ministry of presence! This was such a beautiful moment of grace for me and a peaceful memory that I treasure.

There were other times, too, when people I didn't expect—from my former place of employment or my neighborhood or church—would randomly show up to show their support. Just knowing that people took the time to drive all the way to see me, to bring me a little something to make the days a little brighter, or to pray for me, made me feel so special and loved.

The hardest part for me at this point, though, was being away from my immediate family for such long periods of time. I especially missed my little buddy, Johnny. I felt a deep sense of sudden loss having to live somewhere else without my son, and I yearned to be in his company again. After being used to seeing my two-year-old, playing with him, and taking care of him every day since he was born, my heart would just break when he would come for a short hospital visit every couple of days and then leave. I knew he was in good hands with my mom and Dave, as well as other family members, but I sorely missed our times together, especially those sweet daily moments of tucking him in at night, reading to him, and hearing him say our bedtime prayers in his pure, innocent baby voice.

Sometimes Dave would put Johnny on the phone before bed so I could talk to him or say our bedtime prayers together, and I loved hearing his sweet babble through the phone. My momma's heart would melt every time I heard his little voice coming through, rendering it nearly impossible for me to respond. After mustering up the strength to say, "Good night, Johnny. I love you, buddy," I'd hang up the phone and cry for a little while. I realized just how much I loved my boy and how precious the seemingly mundane moments of life are. I vowed to cherish those times so much more when I was back home, and I prayed that Johnny wouldn't suffer too much from this experience or regress in his growth or feel like I was abandoning him. I asked for the gift of resilience for him and enough love from extended family and friends to help him through this time. This was a sacrifice for me that was so hard to give. I had to constantly remind myself that I wouldn't be in here forever, and that this time away from my toddler and husband was necessary so the three other children in my womb, whom I also loved so dearly, simply got the chance to live.

* * *

Despite the hardships, a fun and unexpected break in the routine would surface every once in a while. One day early on, in the midst of the daily grind in my one-room suite, I was offered something new . . . a chance to leave! Beginning that day and once a week afterward, I had the opportunity to take a gurney ride to the imaging room across the hospital, where an ultrasound would be done to check on the babies. My first reaction was, *Are you kidding me? I get to leave my room? And see something besides these four white walls? And see my babies on a screen? Heck YES!* As I waited for my mobile bed to come to my room and pick me up, I anticipated this break with much enthusiasm. I felt like a kid waiting in line at an amusement park for just a few, brief moments of exhilaration. When my chariot arrived, the nurse carefully helped transfer my oversized body to the other bed. Once I was lying down and strapped in, the ride began. . . .

It's so hard to describe, but this ride was unlike any other I'd been on before. Because I was stuck in the same place for so long with nowhere to go, I cherished every second of this journey. It was as though I was seeing things and appreciating them for the first time. I made mental notes of pictures and signs hanging on the walls and details of the faces I passed while wheeling by them in the hallways. Everything seemed so bright and colorful and new.

The biggest surprise of this first adventure was catching a glimpse of the sun as I rolled past a window to the outside. After being trapped in my cubicle of a room in the middle of summer, with no visual of the outdoors, and no fresh air to breathe, the stunning flash of the sun amid a few clouds startled me. The sun was very bright on this particular day, and the sky was a crisp, poignant blue. As I glided past the window, I sensed time slowing down, and I felt the sun on my skin as the light and shadows danced across my face. I suddenly remembered the beauty of summer, the peace of nature, and the joy of my favorite season. It warmed my heart, and those few seconds radiated a deep peace inside me as I continued down the hallway. That moment was a gift to me and brought me revitalized energy for days to come. I also realized how I had taken for granted the gift of God's creation, especially summer in all its glory. I vowed to cherish the natural world every day once I was released from the hospital.

Once I arrived at my destination, I was hooked up to the monitor, and the ultrasound began. I saw my three little ones through the black-and-white screen as they bounced around inside of me. The technician said she saw three healthy babies and three solid heartbeats, and she told me they were all growing well and according to schedule. Praise God! What a journey, what good news, and what joy this day gave me! I rested so well that night back in the confines of my room. God was indeed with me and had given me extra strength that day for all the challenges that were to come.

One such challenge that typically occurred in my day-to-day hospital life was taking a shower. I'd go a couple days of not showering and then get a sudden whiff of myself and figured it was time to take my allotted two-minute shower. It was quite the process to take a shower in my unstable and precarious condition, and I'd have to be sure I had the energy for everything that was involved.

The first step was to call a nurse down to my room and brief her on what I wanted to do. If she agreed that this was a good time, she'd get a nurse's assistant to come and unhook my IV tube. The assistant would leave the small, plastic catheter in my arm and tape it to my skin. She'd then cover my forearm with a clear plastic bag so the IV site wouldn't get wet or jostled too much in the shower. After my arm was fully plastic wrapped and unhooked from the IV machine, I would shift my legs to the side of the bed, sit upright, and carefully stand up. Then I'd slowly make my way to the bathroom, take off my hospital gown, step into the shower, try to wash my now awkward and oversized body, towel off, put on a fresh smock, and walk back to my bed to lie back down, all in a matter of a few minutes. Believe it or not, those five to ten minutes were exhausting. To top it all off, when I made it all the way back to my bed, I would have to call someone to come back to my room, remove all the plastic and tape from my arm, and hook me back up to the IV machine.

I had to consider all of this before deciding it was time to take a shower. One day, I buzzed the nurse and unfolded my plan. She called the CNA on duty to start the process. The young girl that walked through my door happened to be a newbie. She unhooked me from the IV machine, nervously started to wrap my arm in plastic, and began to tape everything down. The nurse's assistants all had their own techniques and ways of doing things, but this girl's method of wrapping my arm seemed a little off, as though she'd never really been trained to do this sort of thing on a real person. She went heavy on the tape, *everywhere*! I didn't say much because I didn't want to ruin her day, so I let her have at it. To be honest, it was slightly amusing to see this girl trying to figure this out. At least my IV site was not going to get wet!

After she finally finished all of the wrapping and taping, I slowly made my way to the shower and sat on the bench inside, letting the water fall all over me. For a few brief moments, I felt relaxed. But as I began to feel the pressure building in my pelvic area, I remembered that I couldn't stay in there for too long. I quickly washed, dried off, and put on a fresh gown. Once I was back in bed, I called the nurse again to send the CNA to get the plastic off my arm and re-hook me to the IV pole.

I'm not sure if she was just in a hurry, didn't know what to do, or was angry about something, but she began immediately ripping the plastic and the tape off my arm. As she was hastily getting the tape off, she accidentally ripped the plastic catheter out of my arm, and blood started flying everywhere. Suddenly in a panic, she tried to stop the bleeding and called someone in to find another vein for a different IV site on my arm. I sat there in disbelief as blood splattered on my bed and on my freshly cleansed body. This was one of those moments that in itself would be irritating, but was almost debilitating when compounded with the other daily annoyances and challenges that I continually faced during my time on bed rest. In moments like these, doubts about my ability to carry on crept in.

As my high-risk pregnancy continued, the doctors became increasingly concerned that I may have developed gestational diabetes. Sometimes this condition can develop during pregnancy around the midway point. It doesn't mean a woman had diabetes before pregnancy or that it would necessarily continue after the baby was born. Most women's glucose levels return to normal after they give birth as well. If positive for gestational diabetes, though, more high-level care would be offered due to complications that could occur during the rest of the pregnancy and during the birth.

In order to verify my doctors' suspicions, I was directed to take a glucose tolerance test that would measure my body's response to sugar. To complete this screening, I had to get blood drawn to measure my fasting blood glucose level, consume eight ounces of a cola-like, syrupy liquid in a short amount of time, and then a couple hours later have my blood sugar levels tested again.

This all sounds like a relatively easy and straightforward procedure. But for a person who is considered a "sipper" and can't even swallow a shot of anything all at once, coupled with the disgusting level of sweetness in the drink, the process made me hesitant and nervous. I tried to follow the instructions as prescribed, but I couldn't get it all down the hatch in the allotted amount of time. The drink was simply too gross, and I just couldn't do it without the thought of vomiting. The doctors said I could try again another day.

After a couple days went by, I was urged to try and complete the glucose tolerance test again. I mustered up some courage and was determined to swallow my discomfort and the beverage at hand. I set my mind to consume this awful liquid at a steady pace in order to complete the test. If the diagnosis was positive, I would need further treatment so the labor and delivery could go as smoothly as possible.

Dave happened to be visiting with me as I attempted this regiment for the second time. He became my cheerleader and encouraged me along the way. At regular intervals, he'd chime in with an "Atta girl!" or a "You got this . . . keep going!" as I grimaced with each nasty sip. As I got toward the bottom of the cup with the timer winding down on the clock, I started to feel ill. I shared my concern out loud, but both Dave and the nurse continued to press me to push through. "You're almost there. Just finish it up!" I sat up a bit more in my slightly upright hospital bed and shared again that I really wasn't feeling well. Dave gently said, "It'll be alright. It will pass. You're *almost* finished."

Despite my feelings of woe to stop immediately, I put the cup to my mouth again to finish the drink as the sweet, yet repulsive smell filled my nostrils and the taste started to make me gag. I began to chug the rest just praying to be done with this ridiculous process. Suddenly, my body reacted without my consent, and I instinctively put my hand over my mouth to contain what was starting to come out. I started projectile vomiting with a force like nothing I'd ever seen! The hand that covered my mouth shielded Dave and the nurse from the shower of vomit that was unleashed, but it backfired all over me, the bedding, and even splashed on the wall, IV pole, and monitors behind and beside me. Embarrassed and a little horrified, I looked up slowly, and I meekly said, "Sorry," as I sat there in the aftermath of what just transpired.

A few moments later, which seemed like a silent forever, the nurse finally spoke up and said, "We'll get someone to get you washed up and to change your sheets."

After everything was cleaned up, the doctors decided to forgo doing this test again and proceed as if I had gestational diabetes. They would test my blood sugar levels after every meal from then on, and based on the results, give me medication to keep it under control.

During my hospital stay, I discovered that I had an important role in all of this. It was literally up to me whether I wanted to suffer the hardships that stood in front of me or not, for the sake of my children. If I decided that I didn't want to live in a hospital room for who knows how long or didn't want to lie flat for days on end or give up any of the usual things in life I'd grown accustomed to, contractions would ensue, and the babies would be born way too early and die. It was up to me to some degree whether these babies would get the chance to survive. I unequivocally decided that I was *all in*, and would do everything I could from my end to ensure the best possible outcomes for these little ones whose lives mattered so much to me . . . these lives I had prayed so hard for . . . these human beings that were a pure gift and a triple answer to my prayers. So, my body became no longer my own, but rather a home for three others, and my sole purpose was to eat, lie still, suffer, and pray.

In order to be able to give as much as I did during this time, I took my pastoral counselor Rosie's advice and saw this time as a retreat. I turned to God more than I ever had in my entire life because I knew that I wouldn't have the strength to do this alone. From my days as a competitive swimmer, I knew that I was naturally a sprinter and not accustomed to going long distances without a break, so I understood I would need supernatural power to sustain me during the long days ahead.

I slowly began to accumulate a few prayer books and a rosary. I also continued to write in my journal during this time. I even had the opportunity to hang out with the hospital chaplains and receive Communion almost every day. I really had nowhere else to be and nothing else to do in the hospital as all of my stay-at-home parent, wife, and homemaker responsibilities were suddenly relinquished. I seized the opportunity to dive into my relationship with God, and I talked with Him constantly throughout my days in the silence of my room and in the innermost chamber of my heart. I talked with Jesus about the small golden gems of the day. I also turned to Him during the times of boredom, the anxiety of the unknown, the daily struggles, the aches and pains, and during the moments of fear that always seemed to be lurking beneath the surface. The Lord constantly amazed me with the things He was teaching me during this time and the graces He kept pouring out on me. Because I had very few distractions in the hospital, and my bodily comforts had been stripped away, I had the time and the energy to give my all to God and really listen and become more aware of His holy presence. He even showed up in *big* ways when I needed Him the most.

One memory from the early weeks in the hospital stands out. After the initial days of simply getting used to the hospital routine and suffering a few minor and humbling events, I was learning and getting used to the pattern of activities. Things seemed to be going relatively smoothly, and I thought I was managing the occasional annoyances of this situation fairly well. I had a pretty good attitude toward everything, and I'm generally a laid-back type of person to begin with. I naively thought that this really wasn't going to be *that* difficult and I would be able to make it through this time just fine. Almost as soon as these arrogant thoughts crossed my mind, things dramatically changed in an instant, and my whole world turned upside down!

Right around the twenty-week mark (halfway into the pregnancy), the wheels began to fall off. I suddenly had a crushing assault of contractions that wouldn't quit, which deemed me to be officially in preterm labor. Since the initial rounds of preliminary medications hadn't seemed to be working consistently, my docs determined it was time to pull out the big guns—to go on a last-resort, highly intense, and super-effective mammoth of a drug called magnesium sulfate to ease the contractions. I had heard about this drug from the research I had done online before I was hospitalized, as well as from the multiples mom groups of which I had become a part. After hearing about its awful side effects—facial flushing, intense sweating, nausea, vomiting, headaches, slow heart rate, extreme drowsiness, muscle weakness, blurred vision, and IV site pain—I prayed I'd never have to take it. The women who'd been on it and came out the other side notoriously referred to this medication as "The Mag." This was the drug you did not want to have to go on if you had preterm labor. It sounded like pure hell.

It turned out to be much worse than initially described. When they administered an intravenous infusion or "bolus" of this medication, I literally felt like I was burning from the inside out. My body felt like it was on fire, and it caused me to throw up. I'd have to put cool, damp cloths on my body throughout the days and nights that followed, and fans were brought into my room and always turned on so I could get some relief. It also made me feel like I was literally three sheets to the wind, and it gave me impaired vision. After this drug reeled through my body, I couldn't read, journal, or watch TV for a few days because I couldn't focus on words or pictures without feeling nauseous. Even though these effects wreaked such havoc on me, the infusion did what it was intended to do. My preterm labor stopped.

After this intense wake-up call to the harsh reality of what I would have to face for an uncertain period of time, I now knew that this would most likely challenge the threshold of mental and physical anguish I could bear. I began to press in even deeper to my faith. I knew I wouldn't have the strength to make it for weeks on end lying on my back, fighting off loneliness, claustrophobia, pain, fear, loss of comforts, *and* feeling like I'd been run over by the Mack Truck known as "The Mag." Everything I used to rely on to make it through my days was now gone: my husband, my son, my home, my clothes, the food I'd grown accustomed to, my modes of entertainment, the ability to go where I pleased, my friends, and heck, even just a simple glass of wine. It was all gone. Sometimes I began to feel like it was too much for me to bear. It was at those precise moments, when the weight became all encompassing, that I had to learn to rely solely on God to provide. Interestingly enough, those were the *exact* moments when God showed up!

I find it almost unbelievable, but *every* single time I was having an extremely bad moment, or the thought of giving up filled my head, or I was given a painfully high dose of magnesium sulfate, God would find a way to enter my room right in the middle of the craziness. Either the chaplain would walk through the door at that exact moment with Jesus' presence in the Holy Eucharist, or I'd be given a sign of encouragement on my TV monitor or on the radio, or my husband and son or another visitor would show up to ease my suffering. This happened so frequently that I began to realize these were not accidental occurrences. No, they were times when the Lord intentionally intervened and communicated to me that He was there, constantly reminding me that I wasn't alone. We were in this together!

*Journal Entry*
*June 8, 2007*
*Week 20*

*Who knows what the future holds for me and Dave and our babies right now? We are at twenty-one weeks tomorrow, and I've heard they have to make it in the womb until at least twenty-four weeks for them to be able to survive. We're hoping for twenty-eight or thirty weeks or beyond, but right now it's one day at a time. I pray, Lord, that this combo of medicines I'm on (magnesium sulfate and Procardia every four hours) will hold off the contractions for quite some time. We want nothing more right now than to deliver these three little buddies into the world healthy and hearty and whole. We'll do and are doing whatever we can to get there.*

*I'm starting to finally learn what it means to sacrifice for another—to love someone so much that you are willing to give everything . . . your freedom, your body, your comforts, the very life you knew and loved, for months on end . . . so they might live. I used to pray that I could become more selfless and more saintly. "Teach me how," I would say to God. And boy, did He answer! This is what He said: "You become selfless by being selfless. You become humble through suffering humiliations. You become saintly through offering it all . . . for God, through God, and with God."*

*I guess I could have said "no" when asked to carry these three babies. I could have said "no" when asked to suffer headaches, nausea, and vomiting, and feeling like*

*I'm burning from the inside out and breathing in and out a charcoal fire while on "The Mag." I could have said "no more" after sitting in my own urine for forty-five minutes while waiting for the nurses to clean it up or after violently hurling the contents of my glucose challenge test or watching my own blood splatter everywhere while getting my IV tubes changed.*

*I could say "no," but so far I've had the courage, by God's presence within me, to say "yes" to the sacrifices being asked. I am learning the way to selflessness.*

*But please, O Lord, help me not to become arrogant or proud along the way. Keep me humble enough to stay grounded and courageous enough to keep saying "yes" no matter what the cost. I've always admired the saints and martyrs for giving up their very lives for the sake of another or for their faith. I never really thought I'd get the chance to do something similar. I really feel, though, that I've been given this opportunity to do something very courageous for not only one, but three others! Wow! What a gift!*

*I love you,*
*Jules*

---

# *Chapter Four*

## REFLECTION

*When asked to literally lay down my life and be on strict hospital bed rest, I felt deeply compelled to do everything I could so my three precious unborn babies had a chance to live. Knowing that it would be difficult, but not fully comprehending what would be required, I deliberately picked up the cross of suffering and stepped into a period of sacrificing my own comfort and preferences out of fierce love for them. It was intensely difficult and extremely challenging, but God gave me strength to endure the hardships involved. I also kept in the forefront of my mind that the suffering was for a greater purpose and that my little ones were beautiful gifts worthy of the sacrificial cost of love. How wonderful that we have Jesus, who perfectly modeled for us the extent that love will go for the sake of the beloved. Not only do we have Jesus to imitate, but He has promised to share the burden with us. He never leaves us to suffer alone and even allows us to experience moments of joy in the midst of it.*

**Questions**

1. Have you ever been asked to give until it hurt for the sake of someone you loved? What made it possible for you to do this—or what held you back?

2. For whom or what are you willing to lay down your life and suffer right now? Why?
3. In the midst of great sacrifice, when the cost gets high and the weight becomes heavy, how can you remind yourself of the purpose behind the suffering and invite the Lord into that space to share the load and give you strength?

**Prayer Experience**

*Let's be people of great faith who are willing to sacrifice what we can out of intense love for God and others—and even consider it a joy and a sacred honor.*

- **Praise** God the Father for giving us His son, Jesus, who perfectly showed us how to lay down our lives out of love for others.

- **Ask** the Lord to show you what sacrifices are being asked of you right now and for whom or what cause. Pray for the courage to suffer willingly and for the grace to love so fully that you're willing to pay whatever the cost.

- **Ask** Jesus to provide little moments of encouragement and strength along the way as you begin to feel the weight involved in such a beautiful offering of love.

- **Thank** Jesus for never leaving you alone in your big and small sacrifices and for all the opportunities He gives you daily to generously and selflessly follow His way of love.

CHAPTER 5

# Grace in the Storm

*"Commit your way to the Lord; trust in Him and He will act."*

—Ps 37:5

AFTER EACH wave of craziness, I'd enter a period of predictability when things would go relatively smoothly. On these "regular" days, the residents came in around 6:00 a.m., they would check my blood pressure and blood sugar levels, I'd select meals for the day, and breakfast came around 8:00 a.m. I'd receive medications, the nurses would check the babies' heartbeats and monitor me for contractions. I would wait for the doctor to come on rounds, and then I would spend a little time in prayer or take a nap. Someone might come to visit me for a while, or I'd just talk with the cleaning lady or other hospital workers who entered my room.

In the afternoon, I'd eat my lunch, get my blood sugar levels checked, take more meds, and perhaps take a quick shower, pray, or nap. In the evenings, I'd sometimes get a phone call or a visitor or just be by myself. I'd eat dinner, get my finger pricked again, take more medicine, journal, talk to the babies in my belly and my husband and toddler on the phone before bed, and then pray and go to sleep.

These typical days were full and calculated, but every day was new and brought its own little joys to appreciate as well as annoyances to overcome. Little moments of peace went along with some hard battles. I learned to live in a state of being in the moment, and I felt everything in a hyper-aware state. The nontypical days, which were sporadic and unpredictable, were either a lovely breath of fresh air or an instance when pain, or panic, or fear crept in.

During all of this, my husband, Dave, was my constant human rock, by my side through it all. I didn't realize at the time the amount of stress and heartache he was truly under because he was always so strong and giving when he came to visit. The toll on him was great, however. He just hid it pretty well from me and sacrificed daily on my behalf. Not only was Dave a single parent at home during my hospitalization, but he still had a full-time job and drove a half hour each way nearly every single day to visit me for a little while. Sometimes I would call him on a moment's notice while he was at work to tell him I was having a ton of contractions and feeling really anxious. In those extremely frightening moments when I didn't want to be alone, he would drop everything and come see me.

There were times that my husband could only stay a short while, but if I really needed him, he'd stay even longer. On the longest and most difficult nights, Dave would spend the night right next to me in the uncomfortable chair next to my bed, while a family member took care of Johnny at home.

The little things mattered so much to me, and often Dave took it upon himself to show me how much he cared and was there for me. For instance, one night after taking a shower while Dave was visiting, I made an offhand comment about how I hadn't shaved my legs in a while or had my toenails painted. So, in true Dave Yost fashion, the following day he showed up with shaving cream, a razor, and some nail care items to pamper me. He took to the task of shaving my legs as I lay in my hospital bed. He filled up a bowl with warm water, got a towel, and put the cream on my legs and went for it. It was kind of messy and weird, but kind of romantic all at the same time. He then proceeded to cut my toenails and give them a nice coat of polish that I selected from the three colors that he brought. I felt like a new woman after that and so loved and cared for.

Another time when it got extremely difficult and even painful to lie on the hard, plastic mattress for days on end without reprieve, I attempted different techniques to get into comfortable positions on my bed with my ever-growing belly. After a couple weeks, though, I was sore all over. When Dave would visit, I'd ask him to rub my aching body—legs, hips, and back—which he willingly did.

One day, my husband got the genius idea to get an egg crate foam topper to put over my mattress, since he sells that type of medical equipment at our family pharmacy for people who need hospital beds in their homes. He smuggled it in through the hospital lobby, up the elevators, and all the way into my room one afternoon. We placed it on my bed, put a bedsheet on top, and I tested it out. As I sunk into the softness and support it provided, I instantly smiled—this simple fix made a world of difference. I felt new again! It was like upgrading to a luxurious penthouse suite instead of a jail cell, and it helped tremendously with the soreness. I couldn't have made it through without the constant love and support of my best friend, Dave!

More often than not, though, I was left in solitude in my little room . . . left with my own thoughts, prayers, and attitude. For the most part, I had the grace to maintain a positive outlook on things, but I remember times when my mental state was not in a good place and little things would set me off.

Though I enjoyed the process of selecting my food choices every morning, the glamourous idea of having breakfast, lunch, and dinner in bed every day started to wear off after a couple weeks. For starters, I began to wise up to the pattern of offerings . . . chicken or burgers on Mondays, pasta or soup on Tuesdays, a meat medley of sorts or potato bowl on Wednesdays, etc. There's only so much one can do each day with cafeteria-style cuisine that would be placed on a plastic food tray. It became very apparent that it was the same stuff every week. Also, after being fooled initially, I came to the sad reality that the quality of food really wasn't very good either. In certain unstable moments, I honestly didn't think I could get one more fruit cup or tasteless veggie down my throat. Breakfast in bed is great when someone you love surprises you with it to show care and concern and to pamper you. It's quite another story when it's required in a hospital setting and isn't always delivered with as great of care or as loving of intention.

On one really lonely and uncomfortable morning, my mind temporarily turned to everything I was missing out on, and I started focusing on the discomfort in my body, the unknown result of my pregnancy, and the general scariness of the situation. Right before lunch, I became very agitated, and the nurse came in to prick one of my bruised and sore fingers for the usual blood sugar test. She pricked my finger, and then I waited for an exceptionally long time for my food to arrive. When the meal finally came, the woman placed the tray on my bedside table and left without saying much. I knew it was burger day, so I took a bit of comfort in that stable fact.

*At least I like burgers*, I thought, relying on this one moment of familiarity and pleasure to help get me through this day. I pulled the tray table over, removed the plastic lid from the plate, and realized there was a bun sitting there . . . but *no burger*! For some reason this disappointment on this particular day completely set me off. I actually shoved the tray off my portable table in a mini fit of rage, and I watched as it flew off and crashed on the tile floor. Food spilled everywhere and tears ran down my hot, angered face. I started to sob . . . uncontrollably. Alone in my room, every molecule of built-up tension and emotion came to the surface and overflowed.

I lamented the hard truth that I wasn't in control . . . of *anything*! I was also literally being asked to give up *everything*! I was stripped down to my core, and it was brutal and so very humbling at times. In these most raw moments, I had to face the reality of the situation and choose how to proceed. The only place I felt I could turn in these moments was to God. There was no one else who could help me. In doing so, I was learning to rely on Him solely for strength, and I was beginning to understand the simple, but incredibly profound truth that when you trust in God alone to provide, you slowly begin to realize that God is enough.

---

*Journal Entry*
*June 13, 2007*
*Week 21*

*It's been a hard day. I was weak, felt depressed, and at times felt I couldn't go on. The residents, certain PCAs, and just little things like not being able to reach a cup, or play a CD I'd like to listen to, or take a shower really got to me today. I am currently on 2 mg of magnesium sulfate an hour, Procardia, and Sulindec to slow/alleviate my contractions.*

*Yet the contractions are still there. Finally, after a long night and bleak comments from some residents, I got a glimmer of hope from Dr. V. Just hearing from him that it's probably okay to have up to four contractions an hour, that it won't change my cervix, brightened my spirits a little. I've been so concerned with every contraction that it's been hard to live. Now, I can relax a little more and just pay attention to when they're more frequent. Every little encouragement helps.*

*It's so hard living day to day in the unknown right now. My mind has run the gamut of delivering the babies right now and having them all die to having three healthy babies somewhere around twenty-eight to thirty weeks.*

*Help me to remain hopeful, God. Help me to put my trust in You. Help me to not be afraid of what's to come, but give me the courage and wisdom to do whatever You ask of me. Give me peace, sanity, and courage—that I've realized today I don't have on my own. Send people, cards, songs, thoughts—whatever necessary to reach me when I need support the most.*

*Thank You for all You've given me so far during my stay here: Rose (nurse), You in the Eucharist, outside support, family and friends to sit with me, etc.*

*Bless Johnny and Dave and my mom especially. Give them peace, courage, strength, and resilience to get through.*

*I love You,*
*Jules*

---

---

*Journal Entry*
*June 14, 2007*
*Week 21*

*Dave came this morning in time for the weekly ultrasound of our little ones. I think we've named the little buddies, too! Here's the latest: Charles (Charlie) Joseph, Grace Anne, and Lily Jane. They are all doing well so far; their fluid levels are good, and they are growing at a steady rate.*

*I've also been having visitors from the pastoral care staff. It's kinda cool so far to meet new people and talk on a deep level while I'm in my room. I never thought I'd get to meet new people and possibly have an impact on them, too, while I'm in a hospital room for months. What a special grace! Deb even brought a prayer shawl in that some volunteers crocheted by hand while they prayed for me. How cool is that?*

*Thanks for answering my prayers, God, and for sending good people and thoughts my way today. I sure needed them!*

*I pray for continued peace, strength, and endurance for myself, Dave, and Johnny. I also pray that these babies continue to grow bigger, stronger, and healthier in my womb.*

*Love,*
*Jules*

---

---

*Journal Entry*
*June 15, 2007*
*Week 21*

*Lord, you are AMAZING! I prayed today that you would take away my fears. And when the chaplain came in to give me Communion tonight and read the passage about not fearing anything that they do to me because You are with me, I knew you were speaking those words to me. She even ended with the phrase, "with God, all things are possible," which is a quote hanging on my bulletin board right now.*

*Thank you for being present to me tonight and throughout today in this room through the people you send my way. How great Thou art! Help me to keep fervent trust in You and Your good plans.*

*I love you,*
*Jules*

---

It really was my visitors that were such glimmers of light and hope for me during this time of infirmary. They would break the solitude of my own company, offer a sense of familiarity and companionship to help pass the time, and bring me a little laughter and encouragement. I loved hearing about their lives and engaging in an intimate way with close friends. The person visiting would typically bring some homemade food or other gift for me to keep in my room as a lingering reminder that I was being cared for and loved by many.

A few of these special visits are etched in my brain as they were such beautiful moments of grace. One time, a friend of mine named Molly came up with the idea of watching a movie together—a little girl's night in this new uncharted territory of a hospital room. Instead of our usual night out at a restaurant or bar, she came to my bedside with movies in hand, along with some treats and non-alcoholic beverages to share. It was all so thoughtful and incredibly refreshing just to spend time with her in the midst of this crazy situation. I wasn't feeling too well the night she came, though, and my eyesight was a little blurry due to the medications.

Because of this slightly subpar state I was in, we decided to change plans on the fly. We opted out of the movie idea and spent time instead just chatting away about our lives, my crazy situation, and our two young boys back at home. Her visit brought a much-needed mental break from the ominous reality of my predicament and ushered a hint of normalcy into my cubicle of a room.

Another visit from my mother-in-law stands out, too, as she brought some homemade baked goods one afternoon and a brown paper bag filled with fresh vegetables. I remember being delighted by the cookies and by seeing and smelling the large tomato and cucumber she brought to me. My sense of smell seemed heightened during this time, and putting the fresh produce to my nose and inhaling the earthiness was immensely refreshing and grounding to me. It brought in a feeling of aliveness and growth as well as of the summer air amid the aridity of my sterile abode. What beautiful gifts! I truly appreciated, perhaps for the first time, the treasure it was for someone to take the time to bake something for me and even think to bring the outside in with something natural from the earth. She must have known how redundant life in a hospital can be and how antiseptic an environment.

I always loved it when people brought thoughtful gifts to help bring a sense of home or comfort or just offered me something to do to help pass the time. I received all kinds of items: books, prayer cards, food, toiletries, games, flowers, etc. These little momentos were such unexpected joys and very special to me.

Most visits were planned, but some were totally unexpected and surprising. One time, a co-worker from my former job—someone I never expected to visit—made the time to come out and see me. He said that he and his family were praying for me, that I was still missed at work, and that he wanted to say hello while I was in the hospital. It wasn't a long visit, but it didn't need to be. Just that short stopover made a huge impact!

Another surprise visitor was a friend's dad who happened to work in the area and decided to stop by to spend a little time with me. It was a short stay as well, but his visit meant the world to me. I was totally blown away that a friend's father would even think to do that.

One other notable and unexpected guest was a woman I'd never met before. She was a part of the local multiple mom's group and had actually stayed in the same hospital, on the same floor, while she was on strict bed rest. She answered a lot of my questions and gave me much hope and reassurance that a good outcome was totally possible. She had been on bed rest for months as well and now had three healthy triplets at home. She also reminded me that I could, without a doubt, keep going until the babies were born and that this time would be a mere blip on the radar screen of my life. It seemed like I'd be here forever sometimes, but she reminded me of the obvious reality that the babies would indeed be delivered at some point and my time here would come to an end.

These visits not only brought me a little joy, but also carried hope with them, which I so desperately needed. I realized just how precious and needed friends are during difficult times.

Some people brought spiritual encouragement for my soul. My pastoral counselor, Rosie, visited me several times, along with my parish priests and the hospital chaplains. I absolutely *loved* when they'd come to talk and pray with me! Just hearing the words of Scripture spoken over me brought an unimaginable comfort and a reminder that God was indeed with me through it all. God would never leave me or abandon me, and it felt so good to be reminded of that.

There were other times when my visitors were cause for celebration. There were very few days that were extremely out of the ordinary during my time at Hotel Good Sam. June 16 was one of those days. It was our sixth wedding anniversary, and what better place to spend a romantic evening than in a hospital room! We were determined that we would celebrate nonetheless. It was nice to have a special occasion to change things up a bit amid the chaos and uncertainty of our situation.

Luckily, I had minimal contractions that morning, and it was a low-key, routine kind of day as far as the triplets were concerned. Dave decided that after work he would bring me a nice meal and we'd have a little romantic evening together. Okay, not really *that* romantic, but a date night of sorts where we could chat, play some games, and just hang out.

To spice things up a bit, I decided to freshen up for a change and try to look semi-decent for once. I took the briefest of showers and managed to fix my hair as best I could with what little styling tools I had on hand and put on a little makeup before Dave arrived. I even asked the doctors if I could exchange my smock on this special evening for an actual maternity dress. Since it would just be for a few hours, they thought it would be fine. One of my sisters brought in a few pretty ones I could choose from a couple days beforehand. It was kind of fun to think about something besides the babies and get a little dolled up for a change. I wondered if Dave would even recognize me when he saw me.

As I waited with anticipation throughout the day and prepped for Dave's visit, I received several calls, emails, and even some snail mail wishing me a happy anniversary. The excitement was building. I tried to get myself ready while lying on my side or while sitting up for a few moments at a time. It was difficult, but I managed. I chose a blue-and-white–patterned maternity dress and filled it out quite nicely with my large baby bump. I couldn't believe what putting on actual clothes and fixing myself up a bit did for my spirits. I was actually able to push aside thoughts of the triplets and my barren surroundings momentarily, and I felt like my old, pre-triplet self for a while. I wasn't a prisoner of my environment tonight. Tonight, I was Dave's wife, and come hell or high water, we were going to celebrate our six years of wedded bliss!

As the time drew near for my husband's visit, I grew a bit nervous. I was really excited to surprise him with my new look and give him a card I had made for him. I had nothing else to give him, but I thought those little efforts would suffice. I looked forward to our special time together and being able to eat something other than bland hospital food for a change.

Dave arrived in my room with flowers in hand and a bag full of goodies for us to share. He took one look at me as I lay on my side with my pretty dress and smiling face and told me that I looked beautiful! He came over and kissed me on the cheek and whispered, "Happy anniversary, Jules!" The evening started off well.

He then, as enchantingly as possible, pulled over a bedside table on wheels, set down the beautiful arrangement of flowers he had brought, and took out the contents of his bag. Apparently, Dave had stopped over at his parents' house before coming to the hospital to drop off Johnny and had cooked up a feast for me. He went all out—grilling exquisite pieces of filet mignon, cooking roasted potatoes seasoned to perfection, and even searing some tender asparagus. He spoiled me with his cooking prowess. I'm not sure how he kept it all warm, but he found a way. To top it off, he brought in two slices of cheesecake and sparkling non-alcoholic beverages to complete the meal. He thought of everything!

This anniversary night seemed magical. My IV, the monitors in the room, and the rest of the world seemed to fade into the background. That night it was just me and Dave—two best friends sharing a special meal together, laughing, and carrying on like there wasn't a worry in the world. We could have been anywhere . . . it didn't matter. I was with the person I loved the most.

I needed this night to lift my spirits and remind me that Dave was such a gift, such a great friend who was there with and for me through anything life might throw our way. I was so thankful for this little respite in the middle of what could otherwise be thought of as hell. I was glad to be married to such a good, caring, and thoughtful man. We had a great anniversary!

---

*Journal Entry*

*June 22, 2007*

*Week 22*

*Well, things have been relatively calm with my uterus for a couple weeks now. My cervix is still at 1 cm dilated, which is unchanged from a couple weeks ago. I still have bouts of contractions every day, but not enough to change my cervix, which is great news! It looks like the medications are finally working.*

*We have had a couple close calls, though, where contractions were coming every two to six minutes for about an hour or so. But as soon as I took my meds when they were due, they stopped.*

*It's crazy, Lord, when at my most trying moments—like right after a bolus of magnesium or when I was on the monitor alone having a lot of contractions—in comes the chaplain with Communion. I am astounded at Your impeccable timing! But I guess you are God, and You have a way of gracing the lives of Your people in their deepest times of need. Thank you. I am grateful to feel Your presence in Communion here as well as in the presence and gestures of the people you send my way to visit with me.*

*I pray tonight for continued strength, courage, and perseverance for the long road ahead. Please keep my contractions at bay and my body strong enough to bring these three beautiful babies into this world healthy and strong.*

*I'd also like to pray tonight especially for my pregnant friends and their babies: Katie, Amy, Jody, and Chrissy. And for peace and new life to come to my neighbor Traci who lost her baby due to miscarriage recently. I'd also like to pray for Bill who's having hip surgery this next week, Carol on the food staff who's having surgery, Rosetta who's going on vacation, Amy who's on vacation, and Molly who's on vacation. Lastly, please bless all the family and friends that are on this journey with me as well as all the nurses, doctors, residents, PCAs, chaplains, hospital staff, etc., that are key in making this miracle possible.*

*Thank you, Lord, for the time these babies have had in my womb and for my time so far here. Each day is a gift . . . and it's all from You—the Greatest Giver!*

*Love,*
*Jules*

---

The end of June began a time of transition and brought increased hope that the triplets would actually survive and thrive. Physically, I was getting extremely large and weary after nearly twenty-four weeks of being pregnant with three babies, and my belly had already grown to the size I was when I had my first child. I looked like I was fully pregnant with a singleton and about to pop at any moment! It was also getting difficult to get comfortable lying down all day and night, and it was more challenging to breathe deeply with the babies pressing upon my lungs.

I also had a change of routine at this point in the pregnancy: I would begin to be monitored twice a day now for twenty minutes on each baby to see how each one was doing individually. The nurses strapped all kinds of devices to my stomach for about an hour total to listen to the babies' heartbeats and observe any contractions. From this time on, I was also told that they would start doing growth ultrasounds every two weeks to check on their length, weight, and overall growth patterns to see if they were continuing to develop normally.

There was a mental shift inside of me as well at this point. Each day that I got closer to our mile markers, I was aware that good outcomes were more and more possible. Since I was still trucking along relatively well and the babies were continuing to grow normally, I allowed my mind to begin to focus on the reality of actually bringing three newborns home at once.

Dave and I continued to discern names for the kids, I began researching nannies who could assist me once I was home by myself, and I began dreaming of what this new life situation would be like. Some of the thoughts excited me: *What would the babies look like? What kind of personalities would they have? Would they be sporty or more intellectual? Would they be quiet or wildly extroverted? Would they look like me or my husband? Would they get along with their big brother Johnny, and would they get along well with one another?* I finally allowed these thoughts to play a bit in my mind, and the possibilities made me smile. I would even think about when they'd all be in preschool, our family vacations, and holiday celebrations. What a drastic but beautiful change this would be! I tried not to let my thoughts wander too far, though, because I still had a long road ahead.

There were other times when my thoughts weren't so positive, and I'd begin to conjure up the worst possible case scenarios: *Would the babies be born too early and all die? Would they each survive but have some major or minor medical conditions for the rest of their lives? Would it be too much for me and Dave to handle and put a strain on our marriage?*

*Would Johnny start to feel left out because we were giving so much time and attention to the three little ones?*

All these questions and possibilities churned in my brain as I tried to mentally, spiritually, and practically prepare for whatever reality was to come. This is where my ultimate trust came in that God would be with me and would help me with whatever the outcome. He had been with me so far throughout this journey. Why would He leave me now?

---

*Journal Entry*
*June 25, 2007*
*Week 23*

*We had a rough weekend—contractions two to six minutes apart for hours, so they "bolused" me again on the magnesium and upped my dose to three grams an hour. They also switched me to Indocin again. Two days later, the contractions have reduced again to a few here and there, but they remain. I pray that my cervix hasn't changed that much and that my body can hold on for about a month longer. I'd love to make it to twenty-eight weeks. August 1 would be great!*

*Thank you, God, for all your gifts. Help me to continue on this hard but blessed journey toward new life.*

*Love,*
*Jules*

---

---

*Journal Entry*
*June 30, 2007*
*Week 24*

*We had a growth ultrasound yesterday, and the babies are growing right on schedule. Everything looks good so far. The babies weigh one pound seven ounces, one pound six ounces, and one pound five ounces, which is right around the fiftieth percentile for a normal singleton baby. I also got steroid shots today in the buttocks (for the development of the babies' lungs), and I was warned that they hurt pretty badly (and could cause preterm labor). I got mentally and spiritually prepared and held on to my rosary during the whole thing. Luckily Anne was my nurse today—and an "ol' pro"—so it didn't seem to hurt that bad at all. Thank God!*

---

# *Chapter Five*

## REFLECTION

*As my hospital stay lengthened and I experienced intense hardships day after day, it became clear that I was not in control of my situation and desperately needed divine assistance to make it through. I couldn't rely on my own strength and began to lean in closer than ever to the Lord. Out of desperation, I cried out to God and began to surrender more and more of myself and my situation to Him. As I began to trust in Him alone to care for me, God proved that He is dependable and trustworthy by showering me with blessings and gently tending to my every need. Amid the storms, God gave me a great network of loving people to support me, gifts of hope and encouragement along the way, and a joy that sometimes didn't make sense in my situation. God showers us with grace and supplies everything we need when we truly put our cares and worries into His capable and loving hands.*

**Questions**

1. What are some ways that God has acted on your behalf when you've put your trust in Him?
2. How is the Lord revealing His reliability and steadfastness to you?
3. Is there a part of your life that you're afraid to surrender completely to God today? Why?

**Prayer Experience**

*Let's be people of great faith who trust in God's words and promises to us, especially that He is a loving God who will take care of us and provide for us when we rely solely on Him.*

- **Praise** God for being a good Father who cares tenderly for His children when they cry out to Him and put their trust in Him.

- **Ask** Father God, Abba, to allow His Son, Jesus, to hold you in His loving embrace right now. Close your eyes and feel Jesus' strong and compassionate arms holding you close to His chest. Feel His heart beating for you and loving you in this moment.

- **Look** into Jesus' compassionate eyes and allow Him to look into yours. **Share** any fears or desperation in your soul and your need for Him to act in a particular situation.

- **Remembering** that the Lord is in control and is dependable and trustworthy, imaginatively put your concerns in your hands. Then when you're ready, physically lift up your hands and confidently **put the circumstance completely into Jesus' hands**. Now let it go. He's got this . . . and *you*!

- **Speak** the words out loud, "Jesus, I trust in You. Take care of everything."

- **Thank** the Lord in advance for handling this situation and begin to look for the ways He's at work to help you and guide you through.

CHAPTER 6

# Twenty-Four Weeks

*"Trust in the Lord with all your heart,*
*on your own intelligence do not rely."*
—Prv 3:5

JULY 1 began a new month in the hospital, and another calendar sheet to begin marking off on my wall. It was the first milestone marker to reach in our triplet journey—twenty-four weeks' gestation! This was the first day we were told that the babies were considered to be viable outside of the womb. At this point, if the babies were born, the doctors would at least attempt to save their lives with the help of extreme medical intervention, knowing that now there was a small chance that they could survive. The next mile marker was twenty-eight weeks when the babies' lungs would be more developed, then thirty-two weeks, then thirty-four, etc. There was also a birthday to celebrate on this day . . . mine!

From morning until evening, my birthday was amazing! It started off with some of my favorite people stopping by for a visit. My husband and toddler burst into my room early that morning with a great big "*Happy birthday,*

*Mommy*!" It was so cute and got my day started off in the best way. Johnny climbed up onto my bed with a big, colorful bag with a special gift in it for me. I took out the bright tissue paper, with Johnny's assistance, and pulled out a soft, furry white teddy bear with a hint of pink mixed in. The stuffed animal had soft brown eyes, like Johnny's, and a pink nose that was sewed on with thread. I gave it a hug and told Johnny I loved it. Little did I know at first glance that this wasn't just an ordinary stuffed bear bought from a superstore. This bear was handcrafted with love by Johnny (and a little help from Dave), at the Build-a-Bear specialty shop. Johnny had picked out every detail of this bear, including the size and color of the fur. It had a little heart inside it and a birth certificate as well. Johnny named the bear "Annie."

The most special part for me, though, was the fact that when you squeezed the right paw of the bear, which Johnny demonstrated for me over and over, a recording of his two-year-old boisterous voice bellowed out, "*I love you, Mommy*!" I nearly cried as I received this most precious gift and as Johnny continued to push the button, making his voice resound again and again. I knew I would be listening to his sweet, joyful voice every night before I went to bed, and even several times a day when I needed a little pick-me-up. It would almost be like my boy was right there with me. What an incredibly thoughtful and beautiful gift!

After they left, the birthday surprises kept coming. Cards and gifts and flowers were delivered to my room throughout the day, various friends and family members called me, and a few other visitors came to see me in person. Even the hospital staff and doctors passed along some birthday greetings and cheer. It felt so good to get all of this special and positive attention at once, *and* my contractions were minimal the whole day!

Among the gifts I received, one from my sisters Amy and Katie was super special. They both chipped in to get me an iPod so I could play music. Up until that point, I really had no easy way of playing music in my room. This would be a tremendous help for me, especially when my vision was too blurred to watch TV or read a book and I just wanted a little music to renew my soul. I felt so grateful to have so many friends and family supporting me on this day and celebrating with me!

Another most precious gift came in the early evening when Dave came back to bring me some *real* food and to spend some time celebrating, just the two of us. For my birthday dinner, I got out of my smock, as I sometimes did on special occasions, and slipped on a pretty red maternity tank top paired with some black shorts. I even fixed my hair a bit for the occasion. As we were enjoying our meal together, one of my doctors came into my room and gave me the surprising okay to go for a short trip outside. I had been telling them for a couple days that my birthday was coming up, and I was getting a little stir crazy. I half-jokingly and half-seriously asked them if I could go outside in the fresh air for a few minutes as a birthday gift. I wasn't expecting a "yes," and I could hardly believe it! Another incredible gift! They agreed that it would be good for my mental state to get a little fresh air and get outside of my room for a bit.

Fully expecting a stretcher to come in for me to lie on and be wheeled outside (as was the custom on my weekly trip to the ultrasound room *and* the only form of transport I'd taken since being at the hospital), I was shocked by the fact that they brought in a special wheelchair to take me outside. I hadn't sat up in a chair for a long time, but I figured since I had to sit upright to eat three times a day, since the wheelchair back could recline a bit, and since the doctors thought it would be okay to do so for a short period of time, I should go with it.

Equally surprising was the fact that the doctors and nurses weren't coming with us. Just me and Dave on a trip *outside*! It felt like a prison break, but with the warden's permission, as though freedom had suddenly been granted to me after being confined to a jail cell for a month. I carefully but excitedly got in the chair—wide-eyed and grinning—as Dave reclined my seat and whisked me out of my room. I was so excited! Together, we strolled down the hallway to the elevators and then went all the way down several floors to the ground level. I was soaking in all the sights and sounds and couldn't believe that I was actually allowed to do this. It felt a little wrong after all that I had done so far to stay relatively flat. But it was my birthday, after all, and this ride was so needed for a little boost to keep me going.

As Dave wheeled me through the front doors of the hospital, the warm summer air instantly touched my skin and went up my nostrils as I breathed in. After spending more than thirty days in the staleness that my concrete walls and recycled hospital air provided, my senses were unprepared for the onslaught of natural beauty that was beginning to overtake me. It had been five long weeks since I felt fresh air and heard natural sounds reverberating through my ears. As I experienced each new sensation, it penetrated my entire being. I closed my eyes and breathed in summer in all its glory. The air was pregnant with the dewy, sweet aroma of roses and lilacs mixed with freshly cut grass and a hint of rain. It was so refreshing!

I could hardly believe all I was feeling and smelling and hearing, and my emotions soon overtook me. I began to weep as though I had experienced the great outdoors for the first time in my life, and the weight of all I had been through up until this point was released. It had been *so* long since I'd been in the open air . . . *so* long since I was outside of a hospital building . . . *so* long since I'd been home. It was amazing just to sit outside and do something "normal," to appreciate something I took for granted for my whole life, and to get a brief respite from the reality of hospital bed rest.

But almost as quickly as this experience swirled through me, I became conscious of the fact that I couldn't stay out there forever and should be getting back to lying flat in my bed soon. We stayed outside for a couple more minutes, and then Dave began to push me back through the doors, toward the elevators, and back up to my room. That little stint of fresh air was the inspiration I needed to keep going. I was mentally recharged and ready for another month! Back to the grind . . .

Dave helped me out of the wheelchair and into bed. It was getting late, around 9:00 p.m., and I'd had quite the day. We recalled all of the excitement of my birthday: the cards, the visitors, the calls and emails, the non-hospital food, and my exquisite journey outside. This had been a *really good day*. As Dave was getting ready to go home for the night, I thanked him profusely for such an amazing time together.

Right before he left, I had to go to the restroom, so Dave helped me back up. Since I was getting so big and walking to my actual bathroom (only five feet away from my bed) seemed to be too far of a journey at this point in the pregnancy, the nurses brought me my own portable commode and placed it right next to my bed. As Dave got me situated on the plastic seat, I had an incredible desire to push. Feeling a bit constipated, though, I just couldn't seem to make anything happen. Then I suddenly felt a rush of pain as I tried to push again, which was immediately accompanied by an alarming sense that something wasn't right. I panicked a little, Dave helped me back to bed, and we pressed the button to call the nurse. When she arrived, we told her what was happening, and she said she'd just take a look to see what was going on. She began a quick examination as my desire to push continued. Almost as soon as the exam began, she looked up at me with urgency in her eyes and said, "The babies are coming out *Now*! *DON'T PUSH!*"

The next thing I knew, the nurse began urgently calling several other nurses to get me a stretcher, notify my doctor, and get the OR prepped for an emergency C-section, STAT! Several nurses rushed into my room within minutes to transfer me to the bed on wheels. After getting me on board, they ran alongside me down a long hallway, holding on to IV bags and the handles of my bed as they continually told me not to push. They gave me the biggest dose of "The Mag" that a person of my size could humanly handle as they continued to run with me toward the operating room.

We burst into the OR, which was filled with twenty or so trained experts in neonatology who would get me ready for surgery and prep the area for my three extremely premature babies about to be born. In a matter of minutes, in between contractions that were literally moments apart, they managed to give me an epidural, lay me back down, and tie my arms down in a t-formation to the table. My husband was let into the room, the curtain was put up so I couldn't see the operation, and the surgery began.

The next few moments were a blur as my children were quickly delivered. The first was our boy, "Baby A." They pulled him out, briefly showed him to me, and then whisked him off to an incubator with a team of four or five neonatologists and nurses. Moments later, our second child was born, "Baby B," and she was rushed by me and taken to the NICU. Within a few seconds, our littlest baby, "Baby C"—literally the one closest to my heart—was born. She, too, was brought close to my face so I could glance at her, but then was quickly taken away like the others. I was left with Dave, a couple of nurses, and the doctor who sewed me back up. It became eerily quiet. Then I closed my eyes.

When I woke up, I was in unfamiliar surroundings. I found myself in a small, white-walled hospital room, but it wasn't *my* room. No . . . this place was sterile—a blank and uncaring canvas, something uncomfortably dull and new. I noticed Dave sitting very quietly next to me, with an emotionless face. When our eyes finally met, we looked at each other, not really knowing or feeling anything. We just stared at each other for a few wordless minutes, trying to make sense of what just took place. Dave later told me that my eyes were as wide as saucers and I had a look of stone-faced shock. I had just given birth to three babies—at twenty-four weeks—and they were now in the Neonatal Intensive Care Unit fighting for their lives.

A nurse came in and brought me some ice chips to chew on and told me I was in the recovery room after having my C-section. She said we might want to think about officially naming the babies and that we could go down the hall to the NICU to visit them when I was feeling up to it. *What? I can't even believe this is REAL! I was just lying in a bed flat on my back for five weeks. I was literally just celebrating my birthday moments ago. I was supposed to be here for at least another month. They came way too early. This isn't how it's supposed to be!*

After a little time and some deliberation, we figured it would be a good idea to officially name our babies. Since we had pretty much figured out their names already, we decided on Grace Anne, Charles Joseph, and Emma Jane. Then we decided to visit them for the first time. The nurse brought in a wheelchair for me, as I was weak from the surgery and could barely walk from lying horizontally in a hospital bed for so long. I had lost most of the muscle tone in my legs and they looked scrawny and puny as I glanced down at them from my uncomfortable seat. Dave wearily clasped the chair's black rubber handles and pushed me along as we followed the nurse down the hall.

I had no idea what to expect as I entered the NICU for our inaugural visit. After we learned about the check-in and scrub-in procedures, we entered the large, carpeted room and followed the nurse to where our children were located. We noticed that there were closed, see-through incubators as well as open-air cribs sectioned off in different areas. Doctors and nurses were flitting about, and I saw parents sitting in rocking chairs. Some parents were holding babies that were hooked up to tubes and wires, while others were staring into glass incubators with worried looks on their faces. We tried not to stare. There were beeps and monitors and computers and IVs. The smell of sanitizer was thick.

It turned out that we were positioned in a section of the NICU with three incubators right next to one another in the same quadrant. We saw Grace first. I couldn't predict what she would look like, but I was not prepared for what I saw. Grace was literally the size of a small bird, weighing in at a whopping one pound five ounces. She looked fully human, with all of her distinct features, but with ten of the tiniest fingers and toes you ever saw, itty bitty arms and legs, and a full head of fine, dark hair. Her skin was the craziest part. It was thin and red and almost translucent as her epidermis was not yet fully developed. I had never seen or heard of a human being so petite and fragile in all of my life! But there she was . . . my daughter . . . and strangely and stunningly beautiful.

Next, we saw Charlie in his incubator. His look was similar. He had the same tiny features and dark hair, but with a cute little face uniquely his own. He was the biggest of the three micro-preemies, weighing in at one pound six ounces. There lay another shocking but remarkable child of God . . . my son. After looking at him in amazement through the glass container he was in, hooked up to all sorts of gadgets and machines, Dave wheeled me over to our littlest one, Emma Jane.

Emma was one pound four ounces and eleven inches in length. She, too, looked like the others, with her red, see-through skin and teeny frame. She was perfect in every way, yet *so, so* small and delicate. We were allowed to look but not touch, because the babies were too fragile and critical to be moved out of their incubators. All three were on ventilators to help them breathe and were receiving IV nutrition and medication through tubes. I felt like they weren't really mine, though, as I couldn't bond with them and touch them right away. There was nothing we could do except look at them and pray for the best. The doctors and nurses said that the first three days would be critical and would be a deciding factor in whether they would live or die.

So we just had to wait . . . and pray . . . and see. Because of the trauma of my surgery, the reality of the kids being born, and the fact that my milk was starting to come in, Dave took me back to the recovery room. I slept for a while and woke up to all four of our parents surrounding my bed. I didn't realize that Dave had called them to share the news while I was asleep. My mom had tears in her eyes, and my dad and in-laws were speechless. They were in shock. It was such an awkward situation, really, but

I'm glad they all came by. What do you say in a moment like this? There was really nothing to say.

After our parents took their turns seeing the kids and left, the doctors let us know that babies born this early tend to do pretty well the first couple of days after birth. The following days, though, would reveal the true nature of how they were faring. The harsh reality was that the statistics at the time said the survival rate for infants born this prematurely was around 50 percent. Of the micro-preemies that survive, many have serious long-term effects, such as intellectual and developmental disabilities or problems with their lungs, brain, eyes, and other organs.

Dave decided to craft an email to our friends and family who were following our journey to let them know that the triplets had just arrived and to pray for their health and well-being. This message was shared with many others who were not on our original distribution list and circulated to people we didn't even know who began praying for our family.

---

**EMAIL**

**July 2, 2007**

***2:31 a.m.***

Family and Friends,

The babies have been born! At about 9:30 p.m. last night, Julie started to labor heavily, and in a matter of fifteen minutes, we went from "everything is okay" to "you're having your babies tonight."

What a whirlwind! They quickly rolled Julie to the OR, gave her an epidural, and then delivered the babies.

At 10:39 p.m., Charles Joseph was born. He weighs one pound six ounces. He is named after both of our mothers' grandfathers (Charles) and Julie's dad (Joseph). He goes by Charlie.

At 10:40 p.m., out came Grace Anne. She weighs one pound five ounces. Grace is a name Julie loves and Anne was Julie's grandmother's name. It is also Julie's mom's middle name.

Our final arrival was Emma Jane, who was born at 10:41 p.m. She weighs one pound four ounces. She is named after Julie's great grandmother (Emma) and my mother (Jane).

You might recall that our two-year-old, Johnathan Anthony, was named after Julie's grandfather (John) and my dad's middle name (Anthony)—a middle name that is now four generations old in the Yost family.

All three of the babies are alive and doing fairly well. They were born on July 1 (Julie's birthday), at twenty-four weeks and one day. They are on ventilators to help them breathe and are receiving IV nutrition and medication through their umbilical cords. The doctors say they will tend to do pretty good the first couple of days and then begin to show their true colors on day two or three. The harsh reality is that the stats say survival rate at this age is around 50 percent. What they have on their side is the best possible care an insurance card can buy and the prayers of a large and loving community. Please pray with us that God will have mercy on their little souls whatever the outcomes may be. What we need now is something only God can provide . . . three miracles!

Julie came out of the surgery well. She's had some fairly typical post-surgery side effects, but is really doing very well. Right now we are in shock, though. This was so unexpected, it is sometimes hard to believe it has really happened. I suppose things will sink in slowly as the days go by.

Thank you so much for all of your thoughts and prayers. We will keep everyone updated the very best we can.

God bless,
Dave

---

I was moved to another section of the hospital—on the thirteenth floor, of all places. As they wheeled me to this more permanent recovery room, I noticed three silver, pink, and blue ribbon-banners hanging on my door. One read, "It's a boy!" and two read, "It's a girl!" It brought a little unexpected celebratory flare to this surreal and precarious moment. This was the floor where the moms stay after they deliver babies who go straight to the NICU. As I entered yet another living space in the hospital, Dave helped me out of my wheelchair and into my new bed. It was a nice room with a large window with an actual view looking out over the city of Cincinnati. It also had a private bath and was furnished with a couple of tables and chairs.

The next few days consisted of recovering from surgery, trying to walk again, pumping breastmilk for the babies' feeding tubes, and going down to the NICU every once in a while to sit with the kids. Someone also transferred all of my belongings from my other room to this new one. It was weird to see all of my encouraging signs from my wall and the countdown calendar that still had two months to go on it piled up in a box. We were in new territory now, and it was unsettling as we began this new phase.

# Chapter Six

## REFLECTION

*When my triplets were prematurely born on my birthday at just twenty-four weeks in my womb, everything changed in a moment. Things didn't pan out as I'd hoped or planned. The situation was dire, and the outcome was uncertain. It was uncomfortable and unsettling, and I couldn't comprehend what was happening or how things would turn out. The only thing my husband and I could think to do was to sit in the tension of the unknown and wait . . . and pray . . . knowing that God's ways are so far beyond what our limited human minds can perceive. Sometimes in these moments, all we need to be is still . . . knowing it's okay not to understand it all, but continuing to trust in the Lord's goodness and loving presence with us in the midst of it.*

**Questions**

1. Have you experienced a moment of crisis when everything changed and things just didn't make sense anymore? What gave you peace during that time?
2. Name a current struggle that you need to trust in God's wisdom to understand.
3. What are some disciplines you can practice in order to remember the true character of our loving God during unpredictable and confusing times?

**Prayer Experience**

*Let's be people of great faith who remember the beautiful heart and merciful nature of our good and gracious Savior, Jesus Christ. May we have the courage to trust Him with our lives and difficult situations, especially when we don't like what's going on or have reached the edge of our limited human understanding.*

- **Praise** God for His goodness and **proclaim** the truths out loud that He is mighty, loving, powerful, sovereign, all-knowing, kind, and has divinely beautiful plans for your life.
- **Ask** the Holy Spirit to come. **Be still** . . . **breathe** . . . and know that God is God. Sit in the silence of His holy and magnificent presence. Let yourself be loved and held.
- **Ask** Jesus to come into a confusing or difficult space where you don't understand the full plan or can't see how things will turn out. Allow yourself to sit with the Lord in it and ask Him to reveal to you where He's already at work. Ask where Jesus wants you to have faith in His divine timing and perfect ways. **Listen** for the answers in your mind and heart, and feel His calm and life-giving breath next to your confusion and pain.
- **Thank** Jesus for His presence with you in this challenging place. Thank Him for any insights you received into the ways He's with you in the struggle now, is at work championing for you and offering you hope, or is simply teaching you how to more deeply trust in Him.
- **Invite** the Lord to remain with you and to increase your faith and trust in Him.

CHAPTER 7

# Life and Death in the NICU

*"The light shines in the darkness, and the darkness has not overcome it."*

—Jn 1:5

A FEW days after giving birth, it was the Fourth of July. In the very early hours of that morning, a nurse came into my recovery room with a serious and concerned look on her face. She told us the doctors requested that Dave and I come to the NICU right away. It was about Grace. I knew it wasn't going to be good. I slowly and painfully got into my wheelchair with the help of both Dave and the nurse. Dave pushed me in silence down the long hallways and on the elevator ride to the NICU.

After scrubbing in, we were escorted to Grace's incubator, where several doctors and nurses were huddled around. There was a makeshift barricade around her crib so we could have some privacy from the other families in the NICU at the time. The neonatologist told us that Grace wasn't going to make it. Then they took her out of her crib and placed her in my lap on a pillow as I held her for the first and last time.

My hands were shaking, my whole body began trembling, and my mind started racing as my tiny and fragile baby was dying in my arms. My husband gently put his hand on my shoulder as we looked at each other with tear-streaked faces. The doctors informed us that one of Grace's premature lungs had torn open from the pressure of the ventilator and there was nothing they could do to fix it. We were asked if we wanted to "breathe for her" with a handheld pump for a few last moments as we said our goodbyes. They also brought in a brand-new, young chaplain who baptized her and was shaking terribly himself. He'd probably never seen an infant so tiny and fragile in his life and it may have been his first Baptism ever.

I was in a fog. The reality of the situation simply would not compute. One thought that flew through my head was *This can't be happening*. Another was *I should pray*. But I couldn't think straight. My mind was going in a million directions. I started praying like I've never prayed before with a feverish cry out to God for help. While looking at Grace in my arms, I frantically prayed for a miracle. I asked for her total healing. I asked that she'd die peacefully if necessary. I didn't even know what to pray for. My thoughts were all jumbled together as I sensed the critical and immediate nature of the situation. I had already begun to feel the heartache of loss. All that uttered from my mouth between the intense sobbing was a string of Hail Marys and Our Fathers as Dave and I looked at each other helplessly. The tears flowed in anguish and disbelief as our little Gracie slipped away from us and this world.

In that threshold moment on the edge of life and death, when Dave and I were utterly beside ourselves in sorrow, time slowed down to a freezing point, and a single picture began to crystalize in my head. As I held Grace's body on that pillow and the tears were falling in seemingly slow motion, the image of Michelangelo's *Pieta* seared through my mind's eye and left a lasting mark. That scene of Jesus' mother holding her son in her lap after He died, mirrored my current reality. Jesus gave me something in that moment that I will *never* forget. He gave me His own mother to comfort me . . . for she knew *exactly* what I was going through. In that instant, Mary and I became united through the bond of suffering the insurmountable loss of a precious child.

---

**EMAIL**

## Grace Anne Yost

***July 4, 2007, 1:19 p.m.***

Dearest Family and Friends,

We are writing to you with deep sadness in our hearts as we lost our little Gracie during the night due to a serious complication with her still-developing lungs. We were able to be with her in her final moments of life and got to have her baptized before she entered God's kingdom. We were even allowed to hold her for the first and last time as she took her last breaths. It has been a whirlwind couple of days, and we are struggling through this with the support and prayers of all of you. One thing is for sure . . . that no life is ever wasted . . . even one so tiny and fragile and new. Grace has forever impacted our lives and has brought so many people together through the love that binds us all. We all have truly been touched by Grace.

Please keep praying with all of your might for little Charlie and Emma, as well. They are still hanging in there and are doing the best they can at this point.

Thank you,
Julie and Dave

---

After Dave and I were finished holding Grace and saying our goodbyes, Dave wheeled me back to my recovery room. We spent most of the day crying, and several of our immediate family members came by to offer their condolences. At one point during that evening, a nurse brought in a pink satin box for us that contained Grace's things—a crocheted hat that she wore in her incubator, a tiny baby blanket that covered her, and some other memorabilia from her short life. The hospital staff created this keepsake box that we continue to cherish to this day. One of the special objects inside was a ceramic imprint of her tiny little feet that is in the shape of a heart. I couldn't believe how delicate and petite her little feet and tiny toes were—so perfect even at twenty-four weeks! The staff also took some pictures of her as we hadn't even thought to do that since it had been so hectic up until that point. After looking through all of these special things, we put the box away as the sadness resumed.

Later that same night around 10:00 p.m. when all of our visitors had left, Dave and I started to hear the booming of various Fourth of July fireworks displays from all across the city. My husband helped me out of my bed and over to the windows of our room, and we opened the curtains. As we were high up on the thirteenth floor, we could see for miles overlooking a large portion of Cincinnati. We witnessed what was the most magnificent fireworks show we had ever seen in our lives, and probably ever will see. Displays from around twenty different locations in the city were blasting off at the same time in explosions of intense color. From our vantage point, it looked like a panoramic picture. Flashes of color and light were a brilliant symphony dazzling before our eyes and popping off in all different directions. It was as if the heavens themselves were celebrating Grace's glorious entrance and throwing a party on her behalf. It was a spectacular sign to both me and Dave that God's presence and Grace's spirit were with us as we gazed upon the skies that night, causing us to even smile a little amid our grief.

The next day we had Emma and Charlie baptized at the hospital since we weren't sure of their prognosis. We called our parish priest, and he came out to the NICU to administer this sacrament for these two fragile newborns. It was a condensed, yet essential, version without all of the ceremonial parts. Fr. John brought a squirt bottle of holy water, and he dripped a little into a seashell to pour over their tiny little heads as he baptized our sweet babies in the name of the Father, and of the Son, and of the Holy Spirit. We were so happy that they were able to receive this special grace. The very next day, Charlie opened his eyes for the first time!

As I recovered during the next few days and Emma and Charlie held steady, I was released to come home after six weeks of residency in the hospital. I packed up all of my belongings, except for my babies, and made the journey home.

* * *

It was a difficult adjustment at home. I was in a strange and bewildered state. On the one hand, I was so happy to be home with my toddler again and to resume the life I once knew. On the other hand, life was *very* different . . . and sad . . . and unpredictable. I just gave birth to three children, but none of them were home with me. One had just passed away. Two were still in the NICU. How was I going to adjust to this new and startling reality?

I had to learn to take things one day at a time. I began the arduous tasks of going back and forth to the hospital every day to see Charlie and Emma, grieving the loss of our little Grace, resuming the duties of caring for Johnny, and recovering physically and mentally myself. I was also pumping breast milk every three hours around the clock because that was the only thing I could personally do from home to care for our two preemies at the time. I'd bring in the bags of milk during the day, and the nurses would put the milk into their feeding tubes or freeze it for later. It was such a strange phenomenon to set my alarm throughout the night and pump breast milk when no babies were in the house. Also, we had a funeral to plan . . .

---

**EMAIL**

## Yost Update

***July 8, 2007, 8:48 a.m.***

Dearest Family and Friends,

We wanted to give you an update on how things are going. Emma Jane and Charlie Joseph have now been holding steady for about a week. They still have breathing tubes, are under the bili lights, at times, for jaundice, and receive blood transfusions as needed. All of their parts seem to be in working order, though, as much as they can be at this twenty-fifth week. We even got to hold both of them recently, and they're starting to receive and tolerate the tiniest doses of milk. The doctors said the first seven days are the most critical time, so we are cautiously optimistic and happy that they've made it this far. There is still a *long* road ahead, and complications could still arise with their very tiny bodies at any time. So please keep prayers coming for their little souls.

On a brighter note, I am so happy to be home. The recovery from surgery and a month of bed rest has been slow and painful, but I'm starting to walk a little better with less pain. I've noticed that I enjoy and appreciate the "little things" so much more now after being in my one-room suite with its brick-wall view for so long. Just going outside, smelling the summer air, and feeling the breeze on my face, brings me such joy—as well as actually smelling food as it's cooking, and eating pretty much whatever I want again. Being around Johnny as much as I want is such a blessing, too. He is just sheer joy running around in his two-year-old frame, laughing a lot and saying the funniest things.

So the trials and blessings continue, each day bringing something new. We are trying to live in the mystery of the unknown, trusting that God is with us and knowing that He only brings truly good things to His children. Please continue to pray for health and strength for our little ones and for comfort, courage, strength, and peace for Dave and me. We love you all and thank you for your support, prayers, and encouragement.

Love,
Julie and Dave

P.S. We are starting to work on funeral and burial arrangements for Grace, and we'll let you know what we decide.

---

I remember waking up to my alarm clock one morning around 2:00 a.m. to start the breast pumping routine. As the dull hum of the machine sucked the milk out of me, the heaviness of everything fell on me like a ton of bricks. I broke down and just started weeping uncontrollably as I sat alone in the dark of night. It was incredibly challenging to keep this routine up without my babies, hoping it was doing some good and praying they would even survive. To top it off, my breasts had become incredibly inflamed and tender as I developed a severe case of mastitis. It got so bad that I had to be readmitted to the hospital for a couple days for treatment. The physical and mental suffering was continuing to pile up on me, but we had to press on. We didn't even have a chance to fully process Grace's death at the time because we were so intently focused on Emma and Charlie in the NICU and Johnny at home.

After a week or so, we managed to meet with the funeral home and our bereavement committee from church to make arrangements for Grace's funeral and proper burial. It turned out that our local Catholic cemetery has what they call a "baby garden" where little ones who've passed away can be buried in a beautiful area encircled by trees. It was totally free of charge, and they were so gracious with us. We decided to choose a plot there and began working out the other details. This was *not* something we were prepared to do or had the first clue about. I wasn't ready to choose what type of coffin we wanted for our small child, or which headstone we'd prefer, or which prayer cards we wanted printed. We weren't in the mood to pick out readings and songs and plan a funeral luncheon afterward, but we did so out of love for our precious daughter. These were the last things we were able to do for our little Gracie, so we wanted everything to be intentional and beautiful.

I asked my dad, who is an artist and graphic designer, to design the program for the funeral. He accepted this duty with honor and put his whole heart into the process. He later told me that it was the hardest piece of artwork he'd ever created. While drinking a glass of wine with my mom, dad, and husband in their living room, together we created a beautiful light pink program with an image of Grace's actual footprints on it. We picked out the readings, songs, and wording for the final prayer on the back cover, and we decided who we wanted to ask to read the Scripture passages and which presiders we wanted to celebrate the Mass with us.

Grace's funeral was on July 19. A few hundred people showed up at our church to pay their respects for a child they had never met, and to offer us support. It turns out that our triplet email updates we'd been sending throughout our journey had been forwarded on to people all over the country. Our friends would send them to their friends and family, and then they would share the emails with others as well. A snowball effect occurred, and a community of people began to rally around us and pray for our family, nonstop.

As many of these people began to file inside the church, we received our guests and spent a few moments shedding tears and sharing hugs with family members, close friends, and even some people we didn't know. Right before the funeral began, and as the guests were seated, Dave and

I got to share a special moment alone in the hospitality room with Grace's body in her shoebox-sized coffin. I will leave the details of that memory between us. . . .

The funeral was quite beautiful, with four priests and a deacon concelebrating the Mass as if it were a funeral for someone famous. The music was exquisite, and everyone did a wonderful job reading the Scripture passages we picked out. After the Gospel reading and short homily, we were invited to give a short, prepared testimony. Dave said he wouldn't be able to talk, so I took it upon myself as my final motherly duty to speak on Grace's behalf. Besides, no one else knew her better than me.

---

**A TRIBUTE TO GRACE**

## Eulogy Written by Her Mother

***July 19, 2007***

It is a holy privilege and honor to speak to you on Grace's behalf. For it is a reality to say that I knew her more intimately than anyone else on this entire earth. She was a part of me in my womb for six months. I felt her move and kick inside me, I knew her name almost as soon as I found out I was pregnant, and I got to be with her as she lived for three short days and hold her as she died. Let me tell you how her brief life mattered and was a huge success. . . .

On July 1, 2007, Grace Anne, along with her brother, Charlie and sister, Emma, skyrocketed into this world, seemingly way too soon. It happened to be my birthday, too, and these three unexpected gifts of new life were the best birthday presents I've ever received. They were so small, so fragile, and so perfect—tiny hands and feet, delicate features, and full heads of dark hair. Only God could have created such beauty. Then, early on the Fourth of July, just as quickly as she exploded into our hearts, Grace's body faded away like the dazzling fireworks display we watched outside our hospital window later that night. One of her lungs collapsed and was punctured, and there was nothing the doctors could do to fix it. Our little Gracie was gone. But unlike fireworks that are sparkling one moment, then disappear the next, Grace's memory and the power of love that her short life evoked are forever brilliantly imprinted on my—and many others'—hearts.

As Father Daly once wrote, "Every life, no matter how short, how poor, or how powerless, matters to God. Every person can be a prophet of the Most High." And Grace was. She never spoke, met many people, or even opened her eyes. Many would say there was nothing tangible or measurable that she even did but lie in her incubator . . . but the love that was generated and felt by hundreds, if not thousands, of people across the country—because of her—is *real.* People we don't even know have been touched and affected by her great life. Even the tremendous sadness and sorrow that her short life caused can only mean that through her, with her, and in her life, there was and still is great love. And since God's essence *is* great love . . . then we have all been directly touched by God's very heart and spirit! What a sacred honor!

As Grace breathed her last in my arms, and as Dave was holding me and the baby, the tears and pain of the loss of a precious life set in. In that moment, I had an image flash through my head . . . one of Mary holding her own sweet Jesus in her arms after He died. She, too, knows the great pain and blessings that come with such tremendous love and loss. I have found comfort in that shared experience with her and in feeling God's love physically present with us throughout this entire journey.

We have experienced God in many ways, but most vividly through all of you. We are not alone in this . . . your support, love, prayers, emails, calls, cards, gifts, etc., are overwhelming and beautiful signs of God's presence among us. You are the body of Christ at work. You are God's hands and feet comforting us and loving us through this experience. You exemplify the true meaning of community and church and family. We thank you, and we love you for that.

We all love you, Gracie. You have forever stolen a place in our hearts, and we will never forget you and the lessons you've taught us. We can't

> wait until we get to see you again. Thank you, God, for blessing us with her beautiful life and for touching us with *Grace*.

---

After Grace's funeral and burial, we were swept right back into trying to keep it all together. We took care of Johnny and continued making the thirty-minute drive back and forth to the NICU every day to spend some time with Charlie and Emma and check in with the doctors and nurses on their progress. Dave was also trying to hold it together at his job as a pharmacist while taking on the weight of the world.

Although we didn't have much time to properly grieve at this point, there were reminders every day that we had just lost a child. The many floral arrangements and meals delivered to our house were a constant reminder of trauma and death, as well as the hundreds of sympathy cards from caring family and friends that we received. And of course, there was that nagging ache in the pit of my stomach that would creep up at unwelcome and unexpected moments where the hole in my heart would suddenly be exposed, and its raw presence would be revealed once again. Sometimes this manifestation of grief would happen in public, but it occurred mostly in private moments—usually in the silence of my own room—when the excruciating pain and crushing sadness would consume me, and the sobbing would ensue.

Life in the NICU began to fall into a typical pattern, with rare moments of sudden joy or extreme worry. Dave and I would normally take turns going to the hospital to visit with the babies, while one of us stayed home to care for Johnny. They didn't let toddlers run around in the NICU. Sometimes I was overcome with guilt when I had to decide whether to hang out with my two-year-old at home or go to the hospital and sit in silence while they slept. Worse yet was to be there when Emma or Charlie's heart rate would fall or one of them would stop breathing momentarily. The beeps on the monitors would go crazy as I would sit there in panic, not knowing what to do. I felt pretty helpless as we relied so much on the nurses and doctors to care for our little ones. Sometimes I didn't even feel like they were mine yet. Part of me hesitated to get too close because I feared their deaths, too.

There were occasional episodes, during Emma and Charlie's first days and weeks of life, when they were holding steady enough for the doctors to let us take our delicate infants out of the incubators and hold them. During this process, Dave or I would sit in a rocking chair next to their cribs, and one of them was placed directly on our chest by one of our nurses. The babies were still hooked up to all of their feeding tubes and wires, so we had to be extremely careful. We were told to open our shirts a little bit so the baby would experience skin-to-skin contact, allowing him or her to bond with us and feel close. They called this "kangaroo care." When the babies were on our chests like this, their heartbeats and breathing would normalize, their weight gain would increase, and the risk of death would decrease. During this kangaroo time, I was also told that the babies would recognize my heartbeat and scent and be calmed by them.

For the most part, this was a pretty peaceful experience for me, though it was really strange to feel how extremely small my children were. It was as if each one was a little bird moving around on my chest. At other times, it was a stress-inducing time due to some abnormal activity that would occur while I was holding one of the babies. Sometimes the readings on the monitors would go crazy, the alarms would go off, and a nurse would have to come by quickly, snatch the baby from my chest, and put Charlie or Emma back into the incubator for some specialized attention. It was a little nerve-racking for me, to be honest, as I never knew which way the experience would go.

Due to the long periods of separation between me and the babies when I would go back home, the nurses asked me to sleep overnight with a small, soft stuffed animal blanket the NICU staff termed a "snoodle." I would tuck two of these cloth loveys into my bra as I slept so my maternal scent would be all over them. I would bring the snoodles back to the NICU the following day, and the nurses would place each one in the crib right next to Emma and Charlie's little bodies so they could snuggle up to it and be comforted by my motherly fragrance.

At this point, the babies weren't wearing actual clothes yet because they were too small even for preemie clothes and their incubators kept them at a properly warm temperature. They were, however, diapered with the tiniest diapers I had ever seen. They looked like mini-pantyliners taped onto their bodies. A couple of times in those early days, when they were in a stable condition, the staff asked if I wanted to change their diapers under the supervision of a nurse. I hesitantly agreed, but I didn't want to harm my fragile infants by jostling them around too much. I was no expert at handling babies that were this miniature. It felt so weird for me to do this activity that was usually such a normal part of taking care of a newborn. I did it, though, to try and bond with them, savor the moments I had with them, and press into the still unsure reality of caring for these extremely premature kiddos long-term, if they survived.

---

**EMAIL**

## Emma and Charlie Update

***July 22, 2007***

Family and Friends,

It has been a while since we have updated you on Emma and Charlie's condition. They are both twenty-two days old today which is a victory in itself. With the two of them, though, it is really a tale of two different babies.

Emma is presently faring better than Charlie. She is eating well and digesting her food well, too. She has been pretty low on her oxygen requirements, and as a result she has had the settings on her ventilator lowered over the past couple of days so she can hopefully start doing some of the breathing work herself. Her weight has increased to one pound eight ounces from a birthweight of one pound four ounces. She is still on some antibiotics to fight off an infection she had, but those seem to be doing the job.

Charlie, on the other hand, is struggling right now. He now weighs one pound ten ounces, but his lungs continue to be a problem, requiring a higher percentage of oxygen than Emma as well as a different kind of ventilator. In addition, this past week he developed a yeast infection in his blood. He is currently receiving medication to treat that, and early indications seem to say that these medications are indeed working. Charlie also has had three seizures over the past four days. These seizures may be associated with the yeast infection if it has made its way into his spinal fluid. If that is not the cause, the seizures may be related to prematurity itself or possibly even due to blood in his brain. They have put him on medication to treat the seizures, which appears to be working. It has been about forty-eight hours since his last episode. We should find out the origin of the seizures within the next week because the doctors took a culture of his spinal fluid, and it will take a while to get the results. After we find out the origin, the doctors will treat him to the best of their ability.

So . . . the babies are hanging in there, but Charlie is pretty sick at the moment. Please continue to pray that their infections heal, their lungs mature, and they grow bigger and healthier every day.

Thank you for your concern and prayers,
Julie and Dave

---

A few days later, one of our neonatal doctors had a frank discussion with us and told us matter-of-factly that Charlie was the sickest baby in the entire NICU, preparing us for the fact that he probably wasn't going to make it much longer. His whole body was swollen due to retention of fluids, and the seizures wouldn't quit. When we visited, I spent extra time with Charlie, knowing the end was near.

One early morning before visiting the babies, Dave and I were in our kitchen at home with little Johnny when the phone rang. It was the hospital calling. *Oh no . . . here we go*, I thought. A call directly from the hospital was never good. I braced myself, expecting to hear the worst about Charlie, and I told Dave I couldn't answer the phone. Dave answered and nervously said, "Hello?"

I heard the voice on the other end say, "Dave, we're calling to let you know that Emma's not doing so well right now."

"Emma? . . . are you sure? . . . But she's the strong one . . . she was doing just fine yesterday!"

"Yes, Emma. She has taken a turn for the worse and is experiencing renal failure. You may want to come to the hospital soon."

Dave had no words. He hung up the phone, and we looked at each other, simply dumbfounded at this news. We decided we needed to go to the hospital ASAP. Dave went about the business of calling someone to watch Johnny and sent out a quick prayer request to our prayer warrior friends while I went upstairs to gather my things and get ready.

Dave came up a few minutes later and found me sobbing in our room. He had to scrape me off the floor and convince me that we really needed to get to the NICU to visit Emma. I was not prepared for both of my remaining triplets to be in such dire straits at the exact same time. I didn't think I could handle this. After Dave encouraged me and I mustered the strength and courage to do what needed to be done, we drove together to the hospital as quickly as we could. It seemed that this long, arduous journey would never end, and the thought that maybe God had abandoned me started to creep in.

Dave and I arrived, scrubbed into the NICU, and then went right toward Emma's incubator where several specialists were working on her and trying their best to figure out the best course of action to help her make it through. We noticed seven or eight IV bags filled with different fluids hanging around her incubator that were intravenously going into her tiny body. We heard them say words like "acute renal failure . . . insulin . . . steroids . . . kidneys not processing . . . antibiotics . . . could be fatal," in a garbled, doctor-esque way that I couldn't understand. We stayed for an extended period of time that day, praying and visiting until Emma stabilized a bit and we were exhausted.

Hoping that Emma would make it through the night, we returned home to get a little rest. So many people messaged us and called that day telling us that they were praying for our little Emma. Our friends' prayers lent us strength we didn't have on our own, and I believe they were the catalyst for what happened the following day.

After being briefed by phone the next morning that Emma had held steady through the night, we went back to the hospital in the afternoon to visit both Emma and Charlie and consult with the specialists who were working with them. As we entered our area of the NICU, the doctors and nurses greeted us with smiles on their faces. Not used to this kind of behavior and unsure how to interpret their facial expressions, we asked what was going on. They informed us that Emma had done a 180-degree turnaround from the day before. They said she got drastically better overnight and no longer needed the medications. They even took an x-ray of her lungs that morning and said her pictures looked like a totally different baby from the previous x-ray. She was so much better that they even took her off the ventilator and put her on a lower-level CPAP machine that would allow her to breathe more on her own. Dave and I could hardly believe it, and we thanked God for this miraculous turn of events! We became cautiously optimistic about Emma at precisely the time that Charlie was slowly getting worse and worse.

Over the next several days, we drew comfort from family, friends, and God's Word. We were allowed visitors every now and then in the NICU, and both sets of our parents as well as a few siblings and a couple of close friends got to see our babies, pray with us, and offer encouragement. Most couldn't believe how tiny Emma and Charlie were when they actually saw them in person, and realized even more the dire circumstances they were in.

Several people gave us special gifts that we hung on their cribs and IV poles: handmade quilts that covered their incubators at night, two special linen cloths from some friends who went on pilgrimage to Medjugorje (where miracles have been claimed), and angel ornaments and cards. Our babies were literally covered in the prayers and support of our dear loved ones, and it was so beautiful to know that we were not alone in any of this.

Right as Emma began thriving and Charlie's health was rapidly declining, the nurses told us they needed to transport both of our kids to a different wing of the hospital because renovations to the NICU were about to start. As we prepared for this move, the doctors said Charlie might only have a few days left to live.

Charlie's body got really inflated as he began to retain fluids, and he was still suffering from a yeast infection in his blood, lung disease, and continual seizures. Dave and I took turns holding our little boy outside of his incubator on a pillow, holding his hand and gently rubbing his sweet back. He was so adorable with his cute little face and dark hair. There were moments when his breathing slowed to almost nothing, and we thought it was the end, but then his breathing would pick back up and normalize again. This emotional roller coaster went on for another two days. Dave and I stayed diligently by Charlie's bedside because the doctors told us the end was near. We even stayed overnight in a nearby room at the hospital so we would be close to Charlie if something happened to him during the night.

It finally came time to make the big move to the other section of the hospital, and we walked alongside Charlie's incubator as they wheeled him to his own little room down the hall. Emma was then transported to a room very close to his. Almost as soon as the move took place, Charlie unfortunately began to give up the fight. They told us it would only be a short time before he passed away, so Dave and I stayed by his incubator in this new room around the clock, holding him most of the time. My mom and dad were able to spend a lot of quality time with Charlie, too, and got to hold him on a pillow several times.

This uninterrupted time with him was a gift from God and a special time of bonding. We talked to him and cried a lot and said our goodbyes. We even had the privilege of holding him as he breathed his last breath, as we did with Grace. Charlie lived a little over a month and died on August 5.

* * *

When we returned home after Charlie passed away and before we shared the news with anyone, I discovered a small package sitting on my porch. It was a surprising gift from a friend, and I went up to my bedroom to open it alone. After carefully opening the package, I discovered that it was a ceramic, decorative box with the word HOPE engraved on it, as well as some inspiring words from

Scripture: "But those who hope in the Lord will renew their strength. They will soar on wings like eagles; They will run and not grow weary; they will walk and not be faint" (Is 40:31) and "Find rest, O my soul, in God alone; my hope comes from Him. He alone is my rock and my salvation" (Ps 62:5-6).

These words from the Bible reverberated through my soul, brought tears to my eyes, and touched me in such a deep place when I needed to feel God's presence so close. I was so heartbroken and exhausted from this day, and this unexpected gift soothed my soul and gave me strength and hope when I had none. I'm not sure my friend ever knew how timely that gift was.

---

**EMAIL**

## Charles Joseph Yost

***August 6, 2007, 1:27 a.m.***

Little Charlie gave up his courageous fight last night. He died peacefully in our arms after struggling to overcome an infection that caused renal failure, retention of fluid, and eventually caused his body to shut down. We are so saddened by this double loss of precious life, but hold on to each other and our great God of mystery. Rather, God is holding us through this fog of our limited understanding.

Please keep loving us, praying for us, and being with us through this. You are all wonderful.

Emma is doing relatively well and is holding steady at the moment. She actually has moved off her ventilator onto a CPAP device, where she breathes on her own but receives some extra support when she needs it. She's feeding well and just needs to grow right now and continue to mature. Please keep praying for her, too.

God bless you all,
Julie and Dave

---

It was time to plan a funeral . . . again. New readings, new programs, new prayer cards, a new coffin and headstone. It's hard for me to remember the details of this time after Charlie died because I was in such a foggy state. I was a bit numb—just going through the motions in this crazy reality that I couldn't quite grasp while continuing to do the things I knew I had to do.

Despite my hazy memory of the week Charlie died, some significant moments and the grace that poured over us, despite our weakened condition, stand out. I vividly remember certain people who attended his funeral: several youth group members and leaders I volunteered with, family and friends from different time periods in our lives who made their way to pay their respects, and a few people who traveled long distances from other states to be with me and Dave at the funeral.

I also distinctly remember Dave shocking me during the funeral Mass as I got up to deliver Charlie's eulogy. He stood up with me and whispered in my ear as we walked together to the podium that he was going to speak, too. We stood there as a couple, riddled with grief and brokenness, as we simultaneously talked about Charlie's beautiful life and witnessed to the presence of God in our midst.

---

**A TRIBUTE TO CHARLIE**

**Written by His Mother**

***August 10, 2007***

In my womb, Charlie was known as "Baby A." We could see him through ultrasound devices, and I could eventually feel him kick inside me. Little was known about "Baby A" until we found out that he was a boy. Dave and I went back and forth on boys' names and literally at the last minute decided on Charles Joseph. Charlie means "strength" and "free man." He lived up to his name . . .

After being born extremely premature, Charlie lived for thirty-five days under the care of specialists in neonatology. He was hooked up to monitors, ventilators, feeding tubes, IVs, and more. We only got to hold him outside his incubator once before he fell seriously ill. He was that critical for that long. And even though we couldn't hold him much, a bond developed that will never be broken. He was our son, and we shared special moments with him.

The last two days of Charlie's life will live in my memory forever—they were so precious! We were told it would only be a short time before he passed away, so Dave and I kept vigil by his bedside around the clock, holding him most of the time. We even spent the night in the small breast-pumping room so we could be close to him if something happened. The doctors told us after about twenty-four hours that they were surprised he was holding on as long as he was. We were given the gift of *time* to spend with our son and to learn some important things as well. Little did I know how holy this time would be.

It's amazing what can happen when we just sit, are silent, and simply take the time to *be* with someone else. This was pure, quality time when there was nowhere else to go, we weren't in a hurry, and our only focus was to be present to our sick little child. No words were needed, and yet the presence of God manifested itself. You could actually feel God's Spirit as we got to hold this precious little boy—this life that was a pure gift from God. We just looked at him in awe, and every time he squirmed or moved, it brought us sheer joy. I'll never forget him squeezing my finger, holding on to his mommy, like he was going to live for a long time. Even though he was on many medications for his infections and pain, he mustered up the strength to hold my hand. And in the moments right before he died, as we held him for the last time, he fought hard for about ten minutes without the help of all the tubes and devices so we could be with him some more. Even though his body was so weak, Charlie's strong spirit and connection to the Divine were apparent throughout his short life.

I'm so grateful for the gift of time God gave us to be with Charlie. It was a sacred time. So few people get the privilege of holding their children as they die and are able to honor them once they're gone. I don't know why we were chosen for this burden and this honor, yet here we are. All we know is that God is a mystery, and we are not privy to all His ways. We do know, though, that His ways are good, and that *all* things and *all* circumstances can lead to holiness and great love. It is so true that God is made perfect and seen clearly through weakness, suffering, lowliness, and humility.

As Charlie's name suggests, he is now a "free man," soaring in the heavens with the angels and saints. I picture him reunited with Grace, and frolicking with her in the most glorious place. I will miss them both, but am grateful for the time I had with them.

We love you, Charlie . . . our darling little boy.
We will never forget you. It will be such a sweet
moment when we meet and embrace again.
Thank you, God, for this little while...

---

The last thing I remember from Charlie's funeral Mass is singing the final hymn as our son's body was being taken out to its final resting place. Though Dave and I picked out the song, "How Can I Keep from Singing" by Robert Lowry, I was struck by the lyrics as if hearing them and understanding them for the first time. Between the feelings of sorrow and despair, a hint of hope and joy was still there. The whole congregation sang out together:

*My life flows on in endless song;*
*Above earth's lamentation,*
*I catch the sweet, though far-off hymn*
*That hails a new creation.*

*Refrain:*
*No storm can shake my inmost calm*
*While to that Rock I'm clinging;*
*Since Christ is Lord of heav'n and earth,*
*How can I keep from singing?*

*Through all the tumult and the strife,*
*I hear that music ringing;*
*It finds an echo in my soul—*
*How can I keep from singing?*

*What though my joys and comforts die?*
*I know my Savior liveth;*
*What though the darkness gather round?*
*Songs in the night He giveth.*

*The peace of Christ makes fresh my heart,*
*A fountain ever springing!*
*All things are mine since I am His—*
*How can I keep from singing?*

# Chapter Seven

## REFLECTION

*As my world unraveled and I suffered through the agony of losing two of my precious children, God revealed the depths of His love for me as I clung desperately to Him. I became acutely aware that I wasn't alone in this tragedy, and I began to see things in the darkness that I couldn't otherwise perceive. God did not abandon me. On the contrary, in my most fragile moments, the Lord was closer than ever, giving me little glimmers of hope as constant reminders of His presence and love for me. Jesus sent me His mother in a holy vision, a community of supporters, timely gifts, His own words from Scripture, and precious moments with special people. These blessings strengthened me and reminded me to keep directing my focus on Jesus and holding firmly to the hope that is found in Him alone.*

*Sickness, fear, and heartbreak have nothing on Jesus. Even death has no hold on Him! Let us cling tightly to the Lord in our times of trouble and not look away. Let us have a solid understanding in the depths of our souls that God is good and is in control.*

**Questions**

1. How can you sit in the tension of experiencing the anguish of your Good Friday and Holy Saturday moments, while at the same time knowing with an unyielding certainty that the glory of Easter Sunday is coming?
2. What beautiful things has God revealed to you that you could only see during a period of intense darkness?
3. When all hope seems lost and the storms in your life are raging, what are some ways you can look to Jesus and even learn to praise Him in moments of fear and chaos?

**Prayer Experience**

*Let's be people of great faith who hold fast to the light, hope, and promises of our Lord Jesus Christ—especially in times of deep distress, when feeling the heartache of loss, or experiencing crippling fear. He alone is our hope and salvation!*

- **Praise** God for never abandoning His children in their hour of need.

- **Acknowledge** a problem that is raging and allow yourself to feel it deeply**. Honestly share** every concern, fear, worry, and emotion with the Lord.

- When you're ready, look away from the frenzied storm and **lock eyes with Jesus**. He commands the winds and the seas to obey, and they do. All creation is under His authority. Hold tightly to Jesus, to His love and strength, and do not look away. Allow His calming and peaceful presence to consume you and settle into your soul.

- **Thank** Jesus for this time together. Thank Him for His peace that surpasses all understanding and even for this trial that is leading you closer to His sacred heart.

## CHAPTER 8

# Homecoming

*"At dusk weeping comes for the night;*
*but at dawn there is rejoicing."*

—Ps 30:6

THE FEW weeks after Charlie's death flowed in a precarious pattern: two steps forward and one step back. Dave and I would take turns visiting Emma daily in the NICU while again trying to get back to a routine with Johnny and Dave's work schedule back at home. Numbness, mixed in with sadness about the past and anxiety regarding the future, were my new companions as I walked day by day through this new reality. Tiny doses of hope would insert themselves into this new landscape, though, as Emma grew stronger each day. Despite her slow but encouraging progress, my feeble heart wouldn't yet allow me to hold on too tightly to the promise of a future with her in it.

During this new season, Dave and I were given more opportunities to care for little Emma ourselves as she gained weight and strength in the hospital. Having the constant help and supervision of the nurses and doctors was such a blessing and comfort. We would not have known what to do in so many situations without them teaching and coaching us. I remember one nurse telling us that babies at this stage are resilient and not to be afraid to touch them. I guess I was still showing signs of being hesitant, and needed that reassurance to know it was indeed okay to touch my little child at this point.

At the end of August, we had a few things to celebrate.

---

**EMAIL**

## Two Pound Party

***August 23, 2007***

Hello everyone. Good news to share . . . Emma is doing well and has reached a couple of milestones. First, she has reached the two-pound mark, which is a big deal for her since she started at one pound four ounces (and dipped down to one pound two ounces at one point). We're having a "Two Pound Party" as we write!

Second, she is now off her CPAP ventilator and is now breathing on her own with just a nasal cannula (a tube under the nose much like the ones an adult would wear) to give her a little more oxygen if she needs it. And third, she met her big brother, Johnny, for the first time today. He said "Hi, Emma," to her and talked about wanting her to come home. Johnny has asked about meeting Grace and Charlie, too. We've told him that God wanted them to live with Him in heaven right now, and that he'll get to meet them when he gets there.

Anyway . . . it's nice to have some good news to share. Thank you for all your prayers for Emma and our family. We really feel that your prayers are helping our little girl to thrive. Please celebrate her successes with us and continue to pray because Emma still has a lot of growing to do before she can come home. We're hoping to bring her home sometime in October. She's a living miracle!

Peace,
Julie and Dave

---

During the month of September, Emma slowly but surely grew bigger and stronger, and proved to be quite the little fighter as she battled through so much during her short life. She even started to get some cheeks! When not asleep, Emma started moving around like crazy in her incubator, had moments of serious alertness, and began to look around curiously with her big, dark eyes. She began to get the sucking motion down, too, and even slurped down five milligrams of breast milk from a bottle for the first time during this month. Dave and I began to hold her a lot more, hear her cries, change her diapers, and watch her being weaned from her oxygen flow. She still had occasional episodes when she'd forget to breathe or choked on some milk or snot and needed intervention, but we started looking forward to her moving into a regular open-air crib, getting off her nasal cannula, and eventually taking her home.

As Emma progressed and hope was raised, our routine at home with Johnny, and with driving to and from the NICU, became more manageable. At the same time, though, Dave and I were really exhausted. We wondered if and when there would be an end to this season of uncertainty and grief. We were praying for the day that we wouldn't have to travel to and from the hospital on a daily basis, continue to deal with the ailment known to breastfeeding mothers as mastitis, or worry what the nurses or doctors would say when we'd call the NICU for an update.

One day, in the midst of these blurred moments mixed with fear and hope, I remember Emma having a really jarring episode at the hospital where the nurse had to quickly get her off of my chest during kangaroo care, because she stopped breathing. It seems like such a little incident in the grand scheme of things, but this was the unexpected occasion that broke me. It was so upsetting to me because it highlighted the fact that Emma could still die, too, just like the others, and I didn't think I'd be able to handle it. The hope of her surviving suddenly slipped away from me immediately after that experience, and dread was all I felt. Something in me snapped in that moment, and I became so unsettled with the long suffering I'd endured that grief, anger, and fear began to overtake me. I left the hospital in a bitter and depressed state.

When I got home, I went straight up to my bedroom with a heaviness I'd never felt before in my life, and I closed the door. And then I lost it. "*No! . . . No! . . . No!*" I started screaming aloud. The fury of the storm and the weight of this burden started to crush me and take my breath away. I broke down and released an epic cry to God from the depths of my soul. "*NO!*" I yelled out loud, with both of my hands on my dresser for support as I looked straight in the mirror and the tears started to flow.

In perhaps the most honest, raw, and naked prayer I'd ever uttered, the floodgates were unleashed, and my battered heart lashed out in anguish in the form of heavy, choking, broken sobs: "*No*, Lord, *No!* I can't take *any* more . . . I just buried two of my children . . . I am *so weary* . . . I *can't* keep doing this! *No*, Lord! . . . I literally *cannot* take it if Emma dies, too! I *won't* be able to go on!"

I just wept as I reached the precipice of all I could stand. I had the feeling of being on the edge of sanity—pushed to the farthest limit of what I could humanly endure. I had a profound understanding that if Emma died, too, I would fall off into the abyss; I would not be able to withstand the pressure of it all and would explode on impact. I simply could not bear any more weight, and it was up to God's discretion from here. There was nothing else I could do. I had given everything I had. I had absolutely nothing left to give. It was totally in God's hands now.

In a semi-dull state the following morning, I somehow gathered the strength to perform my motherly duty and visit Emma again. I was determined to make it a short visit, though, and I decided to take a much-needed break from the NICU that day. As I went through the double doors at the entrance of the hospital, I walked down the main hallway to the elevators as I'd done so many times before. Before I got to the elevators, though, I noticed a balloon in the shape of a giant rainbow escaping the gift shop and coming toward me. I didn't think much of it at the time. I went up to Emma's floor, entered the NICU, and stopped by her crib for a visit. Emma was holding steady, so I only stayed for about an hour and then left. During this time, I concocted a plan to do something fun with Johnny and take him on a little outing later on this beautiful day.

I decided some fresh air would do me some good, so I took my son to one of our local parks with a spray fountain where children could play. As he was running through the water on the splash pad, he noticed something amazing and urgently wanted me to see it, too. He ran over to me dripping wet and pointed to the fountain and said, "Mommy, mommy, do you see the rainbow over there?" He showed me where a rainbow was visible as the sun shone through one section of the spraying water. I saw the rainbow, and then instantly recalled the one in the hospital I had seen on the balloon earlier that day.

Later that very same night, Johnny was watching a cartoon show on TV with one of his little friends while I was doing the dishes. The boys suddenly started shaking with laughter and talking about the rainbow that was on TV.

*Okay, now this is getting a little weird*, I thought. I looked at the TV and saw yet another rainbow. That made *three* rainbows on the same day! Still not really understanding the significance of this, I went to bed that night and woke up the next morning right after having a vivid dream with the most epic rainbow I had ever seen! The colors were so rich and vibrant that they were burned in my memory . . . brilliant orange, deep indigo, lush green. The colors were so bright and bold!

I finally realized that God was desperately trying to tell me something. Not typically seeing rainbows, and especially not seeing four within a twenty-four-hour period, I figured that this must be some sort of sign. *Okay, God,* I thought. *What message are you trying to send me? This isn't just a coincidence anymore.*

To try and get some clarity, I got out my Bible and looked up the passage in the Book of Genesis about Noah, the flood, and the rainbow he received as a sign. When I read the line in the passage about how God promised Noah that he would never destroy the earth by such devastation again, I instantly felt God saying to me that He would not take them all—meaning that all of my babies would not die, not now. I had a sense of *knowing* through this sign and these words that Emma was going to be okay. God was trying to communicate to me that the rainbow of hope and relief was here, that the flood of chaos and destruction would be ending soon, and that a beautiful miracle of new life was on the horizon. Once I accepted this message in my heart, tears of gratitude came, and I felt a hope and a lightness and a peace I had not felt in a long time. From that moment on, I perceived in the deepest part of my being that Emma Jane would survive and eventually come home.

* * *

Emma continued to make good progress over the next couple weeks. Then came a slight chill in the air as the calendar page turned to October. Emma had now been in the NICU for three months, going on four, and she was the single survivor of her triplet team. She began to grow at a more rapid rate and seemed to be progressing well at around four pounds. She even started to wear the smallest of preemie clothes!

There was talk that Emma could come home in a couple of weeks if she stayed steady on this path. The thought of taking her home was exhilarating and frightening all at the same time. She still wouldn't always drink from her bottle, she needed breathing support from time to time, and her heart rate would drop every now and then, sending us into a panic as the doctors would quickly come over to do their doctor magic to bring her back.

During the second week of October, though, we began serious conversations with the NICU specialists about Emma being discharged from the hospital. For some reason, I hadn't really thought through the idea of actually getting to take her home after everything that we'd been through. We were living so day by day at this point that I couldn't believe this possibility was upon us. My four-month-early, premature babies had only known life within the walls of a hospital with the help of medical professionals. We only saw our babies for a couple of hours every day, and the rest of the day they were being cared for by others. We felt totally inadequate to care for our still-fragile preemie, Emma, on our own. Nonetheless, they told us to get clothes, diapers, and a car seat ready and prepare for life with her at home. I could hardly even picture putting Emma in a car seat, let alone driving her anywhere. But we slowly warmed up to this idea and began stocking up little by little on preemie baby items—tiny pacifiers, the smallest diapers known to man, and doll-sized clothes to fit her petite frame.

As we made plans for her at-home care and outside therapy to combat low muscle tone and possible long-term hearing, breathing, and other neurological and developmental problems, it finally happened.

On October 26, 2007, after 117 days of life in the hospital and weighing five pounds six ounces, Emma officially graduated from the NICU and received the doctors' clearance to come home. On that day, we put Emma in a cute outfit that was slightly too big, packed up all of our things, and said goodbye to life as we knew it with the doctors and nurses who had become like family. We left the sanitized world of neonatal intensive care, with its incubators, monitors, and the endless beeping of machines. We gathered all our feeding and therapy instructions, and then Dave and I nestled Emma in her car seat and walked right out the doors—this time with one of our babies in tow. My husband and I kept looking at each other incredulously as we made our way to the car. We also kept looking down to make sure Emma was actually there with us—and that she was alive and breathing, too. Our new life with Emma Jane at home was about to begin!

I wish I could say that the struggle was now over and it was smooth sailing from that point on, but a new level of care, concerns, and issues began to arise. We still didn't know what the long-term effects of Emma's extreme prematurity would have on her life. *Would she be able to hear? Would she have chronic lung issues due to being on a ventilator for so long? Would she have physical or mental delays? Would we even know how to care for her without help?* These questions, that could only be answered in time, lingered in our minds as we entered this new phase of life with Emma. However, the last question was answered right away.

Just two hours after bringing Emma into our house from the hospital, taking some initial pictures of her homecoming, and getting her reacquainted with her big brother, we tried to feed her on our own. She wouldn't take her bottle. She wanted nothing to do with it and started choking on her milk like she sometimes did in the hospital right before she'd stop breathing.

Starting to get a little nervous, Dave and I took turns trying to feed her using all the tools and tips we practiced in the NICU. She still wasn't having it. *Was it the new environment? Did she sense that we were anxious? Did she know that the professionals weren't around?* We started to panic at the thought that we couldn't even do the most basic of tasks and feed our child on our own. And the one thing that this child needed was to eat and keep growing! We started to wonder if we'd have to drive her right back to the hospital and tell them we just couldn't do it without them. Then Dave decided to call the NICU and ask them what we should do. The nurse who answered told us just to wait it out a bit and call back if she was still having trouble by the end of the day.

While growing more concerned as Emma still wasn't eating, I told Dave that I wished we could have someone to help us out just for a little bit as we got our bearings at home. Literally moments later, the phone rang. It was MaryKay, a friend of the family who just happened to be a retired NICU nurse. She wanted to check in and see how we were all doing because she heard we were bringing Emma home that day. We told her what was going on and she said she'd be happy to come right over and help in any way she could.

Feeling so relieved that help was on the way, MaryKay showed up just a little while later and walked into our house with an air of calm confidence. She playfully said, "Hello," to Johnny and picked Emma right up and commented on how adorable she was. She played it so cool and began feeding her like it was nothing. You could tell she was an old pro. As she began to feed our baby with ease, she said the things we needed to hear in that moment. "You guys are anxious, and she senses it. Emma's not broken. She can breathe and eat. Everything's working just fine. You can do this!" Then she handed Emma off to me to finish her feeding. I took Emma into my arms, fed her with the confidence I'd just been given, and she drank the last drops of milk from her bottle.

What a gift that visit was, and at just the right time! Thank you, Jesus!

**EMAIL**

## Rain to Rainbows . . . Emma's home!

***October 27, 2007***

Well, our little pumpkin is sitting in her bouncy seat on the floor next to me as I write this. I asked her to dictate, but there was no response. I'll just have to write for her. . . .

It looks like she's trying to say, "I'm so happy to be home. Thanks for all your prayers and love. I can't wait to meet you all," but it could just be gas, so I'll share our thoughts, too. :)

Dave and I drove to the hospital around 9:00 a.m. yesterday, filled with emotions. We could hardly believe the day had come to take Emma home. After almost four months in the hospital, Emma was doing well enough to make the trek to Mason. She'd never been out of the hospital, never felt fresh air, and never taken a car ride. We were unsure how she'd handle it all. It turns out she did pretty well and loved being in her car seat; she slept the whole way home. We were the ones who were anxious, excited, and a little jittery.

Emma did have a slight setback at first, though. She had a little trouble taking her bottle at home. At one point, Dave and I were so nervous, thinking it was certain we'd have to bring her back to the hospital. She was just not interested at all in her bottles for two straight feeds, and it seemed like she'd forgotten how to eat. After the nurse practitioner in the NICU told us to wait it out a bit, and at our wits end, I actually said out loud to Dave that I just needed someone to talk to. God must have instantly heard my cry because minutes later our phone rang. It was a family friend who actually happened to be a NICU nurse, and she said she would come over in thirty minutes. MaryKay worked her magic, and Emma took her whole next feeding. We breathed a sigh of relief and felt so happy again. That's the feeling we've had the most . . . happiness . . . and joy! I told Dave that I don't think I've ever been this happy in my whole life. I guess we've never been through as much as we have before, either. The suffering just makes the joy so much sweeter!

Life here at the Yost household is forever changed. We have what appears to be a brand-new, healthy baby, even though she's nearly four months old. Johnny is happy she's home, but he's already showing signs of jealousy and regression as he tests out what this new life might mean for him. But all in all, life is grand! The population on our street has increased by one, and our love has increased a thousand times over. We have been so blessed by your prayers and love, and the miracle that is Emma Jane! She's a beautiful little girl!

With all our love and thanks,
Julie, Dave, Johnny, and Emma

---

# Chapter Eight

## REFLECTION

*After reaching the point of all I could bear of the longtime pain, suffering, and agony I endured during this trial, the Lord finally gave me a reprieve. A brilliant rainbow ushered in a new season of not only relief, but radiant joy! God allowed Dave and me the gift of witnessing the miracle of our totally restored baby we finally got to bring home. It was a time of intense happiness, celebration, and gratitude. The suffering we experienced made the joy so much sweeter! God is always creating something new, something beautiful, something good. If it doesn't look this way in your life right now, don't worry. The glory is coming! Hold on. Your rainbow is just around the corner!*

**Questions**

1. What miracles have you seen God work in your life?
2. How can you celebrate and thank the Lord every day for the beautiful ways He is intervening and blessing your family, your work, and your friends?
3. How has suffering allowed you to more deeply appreciate the good things in your life?

**Prayer Experience**

*Let's be people of great faith who remember that we have a powerful and wonder-working God, and give thanks and rejoice in every blessing He bestows upon us.*

- **Praise God** for His resurrection power and awe-inspiring nature!
- **Ask** the Lord to reveal specific instances in which He has granted you incredible, joy-filled, or miraculous moments when you've tasted the glory of heaven. Revel in the warmth of these feelings and memories.
- **Thank God** for these times when He's allowed you to experience His incredible and radiant glory. Take a few moments to celebrate and rejoice in how good God has been and continues to be in your life.
- **Remember** that what God has done before, He can do again!
- **Let** the Lord know of any current places that are still in need of restoration, and trust that if it's not good, He's not done working on it yet. Cry out to Jesus and ask Him to show you His mercy and love—and expect the miraculous in His perfect timing!
- **Thank God** for the joy you've already experienced, and for the joy that's on its way!

CHAPTER 9

# Grief and Glory

*"We know that all things work for good for those who love God."*

—Rom 8:28

THE EARLY days with Emma at home were quite the transition. Monitoring her health and progress while taking care of Johnny was kind of messy at first, as we fumbled our way through. I remember sleeping on the carpet in Emma's bedroom next to her crib during those first few weeks to make sure we could hear her breathing, and be there to help her if she was in any sort of distress. We felt like we were walking on eggshells at first, not knowing how she'd be or if she would exhibit developmental delays or significant health issues.

It was also RSV season during those first few months with Emma at home. We were told that she was in the high-risk category for developing severe symptoms, due to her extreme prematurity, if she were to contract this respiratory virus. We were strongly encouraged to keep her away from others and their germs as much as possible, and to frequently wash our hands between November and April to protect her from illness. We didn't take Emma out much during those six months, except for doctor's appointments, and we had a limited number of visitors to our house at any given time.

Emma's at-home-plan included therapy, where we would consistently work with her to improve her movement, speech, and fine motor skills. We made sure to give her extra "tummy time" to strengthen her neck and back muscles, we'd regularly stretch her legs, arms, and shoulders, and we made sure we would read and talk to her a lot to encourage her language development. The odds were stacked against her, and every milestone she hit as a baby—smiling, rolling over, sitting up on her own, eating solid foods, babbling, crawling, etc.—was significant and a cause for joy!

Our biggest concern was her inability to hear clearly. She seemed to be progressing nicely in all other areas. Before Emma left the hospital, an audiologist tested her brain's response to sound to see if she was hearing okay. Nothing was registering at all in her left ear, and they told us we should talk to her on her right side to make sure she could hear us. The doctors told us that Emma might be deaf in that ear or could possibly grow out of it.

After a few months of Emma being at home under tight observation, therapy, and visitor restrictions, it was time to introduce her to the world and celebrate her life!

**EMAIL**

## Emma Pics, RSV, and Save the Date

***April 5, 2008***

Hello, everyone. It's hard to believe Emma is nine months old! She's doing pretty good right now. She's hitting her milestones for her adjusted age of five months and has even gotten the hang of eating baby food from a spoon! She weighs in right around twelve pounds now and is two feet tall. Our only concern at the moment is her hearing; we're pretty sure she has mild hearing loss. She can hear most things at a conversational level and louder, but she misses the minute details of language, which could affect her speech and learning abilities. As soon as we know the cause, there are things that can be done to improve her hearing. We are hopeful that in the future she will hear everything just fine!

We wanted to let everyone know that beginning May 1, we're lifting her restrictions on visitors and going out in public, as RSV season will be a thing of the past. I think we're looking forward most to introducing Emma to those of you who haven't met her yet, and going out as a complete family.

As a way to thank all of you for your prayers and support over the past year or so, we're throwing a *huge* open house party on June 21 for Emma's first birthday, and my birthday, too. (We'll be out of town on our actual birthday.) Please save the date so you can celebrate Emma's life with us!

Peace and love,
Julie, Dave, Johnny, and Emma Yost

---

Emma's first birthday bash was a huge success, and hundreds of people filed in and out of our home, excited to see her. They commented on how adorable and full of spunk she was, and how happy they were to finally meet her in person. My fears of Emma pooping out at the party faded, too, as she seemed to feed off of everyone's energy. She had a great time, and so did we as we caught up with people and celebrated the miracle of her life! There were mostly shared emotions of abundant joy, but these were subtly mixed in with tinges of sorrow as we celebrated this heartrending July birthday of both mine and Emma's, while still remembering our sweet little Grace and Charlie in heaven.

After this incredible celebration, Dave and I took a deep breath for the first time in quite a while. Emma began to really thrive, and there were no indications of any permanent damage or side effects from her extreme prematurity at this point. We even discovered that because her eardrums were so small, they quickly got clogged with wax and shut off her ability to hear. It turned out that she wasn't deaf at all . . . just waxy! We just had to take her to a children's hospital every couple of months so the doctors could get the wax out of her ears. Once her eardrums grew and the clogging ceased, she was fine—a perfectly healthy baby girl!

At this point, though, I realized there had been little time to grieve the deaths of Grace and Charlie, and process this whole ordeal. I had a profound sense of missing my two babies, and had moments when I allowed myself the space to feel the pangs of their loss. But the magnitude of the trauma and grief we endured didn't fully hit until after we knew Emma was truly okay, a year or so after the triplets were born. I was doing too much to care for my children on this side of heaven to think much about myself and what I needed at the time. But as grief often does when unresolved, it found me and showed up in a way that I didn't attribute to grief at first.

One day soon after Emma's first birthday, I noticed my hands were a little numb and tingling. I didn't think much of it, but I noted how strange it was. A few days later, as these sensations persisted, I realized I couldn't shake them off, and I began to become concerned. About a week after that, an alarming new symptom appeared: my tongue began to feel numb as well. At this point, I started to panic a little, and I began to research what can cause numbness in the hands and face. What I found was not encouraging. Fully thinking I was having a stroke or had developed some sort of neurological problem or the beginnings of a debilitating disease, I decided I better go to the doctor to get checked out. My general practitioner did some initial physical tests and some blood work, but he didn't find anything that would account for the loss of feeling and tingling in my hands and tongue. He then sent me to a neurologist who ordered several tests of her own to determine the cause of my symptoms.

The day of my appointment, I found myself in a waiting room alone, praying that this specialist would be able to help me figure out what was really going on. When my name was called, I walked into the examination room and nervously waited for the doctor. She came in, introduced herself, and asked a few questions about my initial test results and what I was experiencing in my body. Then she started the exam. She tested all of my limbs and muscles by making me do various balancing and resistance exercises. She was looking to see if I was weak in any areas, and if my body wasn't responding properly.

After all of that, the doctor told me right away that she found nothing physically wrong with me. In the next breath, though, she confirmed that what I was feeling and experiencing was indeed real. Then she looked at me compassionately and asked me an interesting question. She said, "Have you suffered any trauma recently?" She was the first doctor to ask me that question.

I looked back at her, and after a few seconds, said, "Well . . . yes. I had a pretty traumatic triplet pregnancy and was on strict hospital bed rest for five weeks. I lost two of my children, had a preemie in the NICU for four months, and have been caring for her and my toddler 24/7 ever since." As I spoke the words out loud, tears formed in my eyes and began trickling down my cheeks. I don't think I'd ever strung words together that outwardly expressed the reality of what I'd been through during the past few years. It was the first time I realized the enormity of everything that had happened, and it hit me like a wrecking ball. I hadn't taken the time to really process any of it as it was all happening. I just had to keep going for the sake of my family at the time. My body was now screaming at me to deal with the emotional turmoil lying just beneath the surface, and to heal from everything I had endured.

The doctor told me how sorry she was for everything I had been through, and said that my bodily symptoms were most likely a physical manifestation of the trauma and loss I experienced—a form of PTSD. She recommended that I start to unpack it all with a counselor before it got worse. I couldn't believe that my physical symptoms were actually a sign that I needed to grieve. It was time.

After that doctor's visit, I spent the next several months in counseling, and intentionally entered into the grueling work of inner healing so my mind, body, and spirit could recover. My husband was not immune to these expressions of unsettled heartache either, and we began to meet both as individuals and as a couple with clinical therapists and spiritual directors as we sought healing. Dave and I had many tear-filled conversations and intense battles as we walked (and sometimes crawled) together through this agonizing season. We began to face the bitter memories, and feel deeply the piercing sadness of the loss that plagued us both. We lived one day at a time, holding on to each other and leaning on our dear friends and family, professional supporters, and our loving God to help us through this dark but necessary period on the road to wholeness.

While dealing with my own battle scars, a counselor helped me unearth emotions and internal wounds that needed to come into the light. I talked about everything and let every emotion spill out. I cried, I got angry, and I mourned my life with Grace and Charlie not in it. My counselor also taught me ways to continue to process the whole experience and cope with my loss. The numbness in my hands and tongue began to subside.

I also met with a dear priest friend during this time who helped me to be completely vulnerable with the Lord. I learned to ask God the questions I needed answers to, and to bring every emotion, concern, and need before Him honestly and deliberately so He could show His heart for me and my children, and begin healing me on a spiritual level. In prayer, Jesus revealed to me that my loss was not a punishment from Him—that He didn't cause my babies to die. He actually felt my agony acutely, and wept alongside me. I came to realize, too, that even though this experience was excruciatingly painful, God wanted to heal my heart completely and use the situation for good if I would allow it—to grow in greater intimacy with Him and likeness to Him, to help others going through extremely difficult situations, to remember the glimmers of hope I found in Him amid my suffering and loss, and to share that hope with others.

Through this time of intense therapeutic and pastoral counseling, and by spending so much intentional time with God in prayer about my trials, I slowly began to emerge as a renewed person. Every once in a while, I still feel moments of sadness when I miss my children's physical presence with me and have fleeting thoughts of "what could have been," but I've eventually come out on the other side, and our loving God has brought restoration out of the ashes. I now have a solid conviction that God is good despite my circumstances, and a firm, personal understanding that God never abandons me—especially in my suffering. I don't have to live in despair or fear . . . because God is with me!

The occasions of sadness have become less frequent and poignant over time, and are now more of a gentle ache that makes me long for heaven—to be reunited with Grace and Charlie and to be where there are no more tears, suffering, and death. Every so often, God has also given me a deep peace about the situation and the unbelievable grace—especially on significant anniversaries or important moments in our family's life—to experience the nearness of Grace and Charlie's presence. I've received various signs throughout the years, when the veil between heaven and earth has been lifted and God has given me a moment of connection with my departed children, when I can perceive that their spirits are still alive and with me.

One of the first memorable signs I received was on my birthday, when my triplets would have all turned two. July 1 is always a beautiful and difficult day when I feel the celebratory joy of birth and life, and the utter agony of death and loss, all wrapped up together. My closest friends and family members recognize this, and often send me messages on our birthday that help me to both celebrate life and ease the sorrow of loss. A friend of mine from church, with whom I was leading a women's retreat at the time, sent me this birthday message in 2009.

---

**EMAIL**

***June 30, 2009***

Dear Julie,

Happy Birthday! I can remember praying for your family when the babies were born. I am sure it must be bittersweet for you to celebrate yours and Emma's birthday and be missing some of your family. I will be praying for you that you will enjoy the day, that you will be surrounded with blessings, and that God will give you some little tangible sign for you to "see" Grace and Charlie (in party hats) celebrating with our Lord Jesus. God has so much good to give to us and offers us so much. May He surround you with love and make *His* presence known to you when you need it most. Have a safe and relaxing vacation.

Love you, girl!
Rita

---

After receiving this and others' birthday messages, and celebrating with Emma and my family throughout the day, I went out to the mailbox that evening to see if Emma and I received any birthday cards. What I pulled out of the box was astonishing and stopped me in my tracks. Right on top of the pile of cards and bills was a *Triplet* magazine—a magazine we no longer subscribed to—with three babies on the cover, celebrating not with party hats, but in their birthday suits. What a strange but surreal and beautiful sight to see on our birthday. As I continued to look at the three triplet babies, a tear filled with divine peace and reassurance began to well up inside of me, and I fell to the ground in recognition of this gracious sign from heaven. Then I recalled the prayer the previous day from my friend Rita. . . .

---

**EMAIL**

***July 2, 2009***

Thanks, Rita. It was a bittersweet day yesterday, but God miraculously sent us that "little sign" you mentioned, to let us know Grace and Charlie were with us and okay. When I opened my mailbox at the end of the day yesterday to get my birthday greetings, there was a big magazine that said Triplets, and had three little beautiful babies lying in their birthday suits, huddled together. We have been unsubscribed to this magazine for over a year now, and on our birthday of all days . . . there it was—a birthday card from heaven. I just cried with joy! God is so good!

Julie

---

Through the years, pink roses and blue butterflies have also been special signs to me of Grace and Charlie's presence. They just show up somehow on our birthday, the anniversary of their deaths, as well as at random times when I'm thinking about them. These signs point to the reality that my children are okay and reassure me of God's goodness and the promise of heaven. One special day on the eleventh anniversary of Charlie's death, I received more than one sign. I was so astounded that I wrote a Facebook post about the events that unfolded that day.

---

**FACEBOOK POST**

***August 5, 2018***

I never heard my son, Charlie, tell me he loved me . . . until last night. Charlie is my baby boy who passed away at one month old, eleven years ago today. Sometimes I get a little sign from heaven that Charlie's presence is with me and that everything's okay. Last night and again today—on the anniversary of his death—I received three . . .

A blue butterfly was the first sign. Blue butterflies always remind me of Charlie. Today when we dropped my oldest son, Johnny, off at camp, my daughter, Emma, yelled out to me near the lake to look at a beautiful blue butterfly that landed right next to her. I smiled as I saw it dancing around her, and as she playfully chased it around. My thoughts turned to Charlie. . . .

The second sign was when I ran into a person I'm taking classes with at my son's camp. I saw her family in the bunk house and went over to say hello. She introduced me to her son, who was eleven years old—the same age my baby boy would be today. His name happened to be Charlie. I loved just hearing and saying my boy's name out loud today. Charlie . . .

The third sign happened last night after our family prayers. I asked the kids if they knew what the date was tomorrow, and they didn't, since we've been on vacation and have lost track of the days. I reminded them that it was going to be August 5—the day their baby brother passed away. Later, Johnny came into my room looking a little sad. I asked what was wrong, and he shared that for some reason he had been thinking about Charlie throughout the whole day, not knowing that the anniversary of his passing was the next day. Johnny never really knew Charlie, as he was two-and-a-half years old when Charlie was born. Then, with tears in his eyes, and totally out of character, he mustered up the courage to say, "Mom, I think Charlie wants me to tell you that he loves you very much." In that moment, I truly heard and felt for the first time ever that Charlie was trying to make sure I knew that he loved me. My heart melted with joy. Charlie . . .

I have been blessed today as I felt the presence of my baby boy near. I have come to know that these types of things are not coincidences, but God-incidences. I hope this message encourages you today—especially to anyone missing a loved one. God is good . . . *all the time* . . . and our loved ones on the "other side" are forever near. Love never goes away.

---

These (and even more) incredible instances of continued connection with my deceased children have brought me a deep sense of consolation, and have reassured me again and again of God's goodness and the certainty of eternal life. I talk to my babies all the time and constantly ask them to intercede for me and my family. Grace and Charlie are our own personal little saints in heaven!

Love never goes away. Love was always with me and has never left. Death cannot ever take love away. God has shown me the glorious and transformative power of His great love in the darkest and most difficult parts of my human experience, and in the great mysteries of life and death that I still can't fully comprehend. Because of this, I am able to live confident and free, knowing God is always with me and can work any brokenness, evil, sickness, or even death, for good. I am thankful for this whole experience, the many lessons learned, and for the miracle of Emma's life that remains.

I found out a few years after we named our baby girl that the name Emma means "universal" and "whole." It is also a derivative of the name Emmanuel . . . which literally translates to "God with us." And so, He *is*!

*Final Journal Entry*

*Dear God,*

*Thank you . . . for this cross that I carried with You. Thank You for showing me Your heart amid my suffering. Thank you for being who You are—for Your goodness, mercy, and provision. Thank You for being with me in every moment of this journey and for transforming my pain and sorrow into peace and joy. Thank You, God, that "in my deepest wound, I saw Your glory, and it dazzled me!" (St. Augustine) Thank You for the miracles of Grace and Charlie and Emma. Thank You for loving me so well during this whole experience and for giving me the abundant life You promised.*

*My Lord and my God, You are over all, through all, and in all things!*

*My heart is full of gratitude . . . and I am forever thankful!*

*Your beloved child,*
*Jules*

# *Chapter Nine*

## REFLECTION

*After Emma came home from the hospital and was doing well, my built-up anguish and neglected grief surfaced and needed to be addressed. In working through these things with the help of counselors, spiritual directors, and prayer, Jesus met me in my pain. He enabled me to process the events that occurred, lament the loss of my children, and heal from the trauma I endured. By God's grace, I eventually came out on the other side, thankful for the whole experience, and able to attest to God's goodness within it. Jesus wept with me as I cried, gently tended to my deep wounds, and brought me to a more solid place of understanding and peace. The Lord has made me new, and has transformed this entire experience into a beautiful testimony of His extravagant and faithful love. Everything we bring to the Lord can be redeemed and transformed. God can heal and make any situation work out for good!*

**Questions**

1. What lessons have you learned during periods of grief?
2. Are there any wounded places where you still need time to mourn, process, and heal with Jesus?
3. How has the Lord redeemed and transformed painful areas of your life when you've given the broken pieces to Him? How can you share the good news of what the Lord has done in this situation with others?

**Prayer Experience**

*Let's be people of great faith who remember that our God loves us so deeply and intimately—especially in times of profound sorrow and tragedy. Jesus has the power to heal and resurrect any painful or dead parts of our lives.*

**Praise** God for His ability to not only cry with us when we are hurting, but to take all of our brokenness and turn it into something beautiful and new.

**Ask** the Lord to show you any wounded memories or places in your heart that are still in need of His healing touch. Ask Him where He was during those painful moments in your life, and what insights He wants to reveal to bring you consolation and peace. Pay attention to what surfaces in your mind and heart.

**Ask** Jesus if there's someone you need to forgive from this difficult time, and allow yourself to say out loud, "Jesus, I forgive [person's name]. . . for [hurtful action] . . ." (even if you don't *feel* like it).

**Sit** in holy silence and allow the Lord to heal you. Let His deepest peace envelop you.

**Entrust** this entire situation to the Lord, and thank Him for the ways He's working in it (even if you can't see evidence of this reality yet). Then, with great faith and expectation, watch what God will do to redeem, restore, and use it all for good!

EPILOGUE

# Viable

*"Whoever finds his life will lose it, and whoever loses his life for My sake will find it."*

—Mt 10:39

THE WORD *viable* refers to something that is able to function properly and even grow. It is made up of the Latin root word *vita*, meaning "life," and the ending *able*, which means "to be possible." In scientific terms, when a plant is said to be viable, it is fully capable of living in its environment—even a harsh one, like a cactus that is able to grow in the desert.

In the early 2000s, the point of viability for a baby was the twenty-four-week mark of pregnancy. It is the first point when doctors considered it possible for an infant to be able to live outside of the womb—most of the time with extreme medical intervention and likely with the child suffering some lifelong health issues. This was the exact point in time when my triplets were born.

Emma is a living testimony that this theory is true, but to an even greater extent. She has not only been able to live, but she is flourishing! She is now seventeen years old and still has absolutely *no* health challenges whatsoever, is on no medications, and has defied all the odds! Though she has her unique struggles and moody moments as any teenager does, she is strong physically, and is on her high school cross country and swim teams. She's very intelligent and is on the honor roll at school, she just got her driver's license, and she has dreams of going into a service profession and possibly becoming a NICU nurse! Emma loves Jesus and is also loved by her teachers, family members, and close friends. Her strong faith, incredibly kind heart for others, and inner joy just shine in and through her beautiful life. She is such a gift!

I've been caught off guard several times throughout Emma's childhood, and unexpected tears have welled up in moments of witnessing my Emma Jane surpassing every obstacle that doctors warned would most likely be her fate: passing her first hearing test at school, getting all As on her first report card, learning how to ride a bike, becoming a black belt in Tae Kwon Do, celebrating sacraments at church, and crossing the finish line at her first cross-country 5K race. All of these typical proud parent moments have been supercharged with significance and grace, because each one is a stunning reminder that Emma not only survived her four-month early birth, but is thriving! All her parts are working. There are no lingering effects. She's been completely healed, is fully alive, and is truly a walking miracle! As St. Irenaeus once said, "[Her] very life declares the glory of God!"

* * *

The point of viability for Emma was twenty-four weeks, but for me, it was thirty-one years. This whole experience revolving around our birthdays was a turning point in my life and the time when I became viable—in the most unlikely of places. It was the time for me when surrender, hope, sacrifice, beauty, suffering, death, and restoration were all intricately woven together, and the place where God met me, smack-dab in the middle of it all.

In entering into these paschal mysteries of my own life during this season, with the Lord by my side, I discovered life in its fullness. I learned that when I gave it all to God and lived it all with Him, He sanctified every moment, gave me strength when I had none, and allowed glimmers of heavenly light to seep into my human experience.

And when He asked me to endure the cross that was before me—to die to my own desires and plans, to intentionally suffer for the sake of my children, and to trust in Him even when two of my babies passed away—God took me to an even deeper place of intimacy and showed me things I couldn't have perceived elsewhere. I found that paradoxical Scripture passage to be true: "Whoever loses his life for My sake will find it" (Mt 10:39). What I found was a glorious treasure chest of grace and beauty that I couldn't normally comprehend. I came to know and partner with the deep love of our almighty God that was hidden within the pain, and was just waiting to be discovered. God was profoundly there—even in the darkness, even in the suffering—teaching me not to be afraid, tending to my wounds, and gently asking me to trust in His goodness.

God never promised that He would take away all of our pain and suffering, but He did promise that He would be with us in the midst of it—helping us, holding us, crying with us, and showing us that beauty and love and hope are still there despite our circumstances. And through my journey, He was!

This whole wild, painful, and wonderful journey led me to a place where I found that love dwells and never leaves. It's the hard yet beautiful space that, when pushed through, is where transformation, healing, and breakthrough occurs. The cross of suffering I embraced was the place where I found such a sweet closeness to the very heart of God, and experienced His radiant glory for that brief season in time.

Never before in my life had I endured so much, but never before in my life did I feel so near to God. It was an eternal and freeing state of being—a truly sacred space. I became wrapped up in the mystery of God and was privileged to participate in it. In the midst of the trials, I felt an aliveness, a purposefulness, and a closeness to God I had never before experienced or embodied. I was doing exactly what I was supposed to be doing, and I did it all with Him. In doing so, I came to *know* Jesus on a whole new level, and He proved to be dependable, trustworthy, merciful, and kind.

And for that blessed period of time, I became more like Him. Or perhaps, more accurately, it was no longer I who lived, but Christ who lived in me (Gal 2:20). There is nothing greater than that.

"The glory of God is man fully alive!" (St. Irenaeus) And to be fully alive—to be viable—we have to learn how to die to ourselves. . . and to trust in *God* . . . because He is good and He is with us in it all!

---

*Thirty-First Birthday Card from My Husband, Dave*
*July 1, 2007*
*(Received Moments Before the Birth of Our Triplets)*

*Happy Birthday, Jules!*

*Wow, this is a birthday you definitely won't forget. You always like to go to hotels to celebrate special occasions . . . well, here you are at the Hotel Good Sam! Okay, so it might not be the ideal situation, but that leaves no less reason to celebrate. Today you get to celebrate the fact that out of your thirty-one blessed years of life, you have totally and completely "died to self" and lived a full month for the sake of others. (Three others to be exact.) What a gift to have had that opportunity, and what an accomplishment to have seized it! Who would have ever thought that "seizing the day" would require you to lie down all day? Well, my dear, it was the hand you were dealt, and by playing it, you are redefining the phrase.*

*So celebrate, my love, for you have lived more in the past month than perhaps you ever had in your previous thirty-one years.*

*I love you,*
*Davy*

*"Then Jesus said to his disciples,*
*'Whoever wishes to come after me*
*must deny himself, take up his cross,*
*and follow me.'"*

—Mt: 16:24

†

*All Glory*
*be to the Father*
*and to the Son*
*and to the Holy Spirit,*
*as it was in the beginning*
*is now, and ever shall be*
*world without end.*
*Amen.*

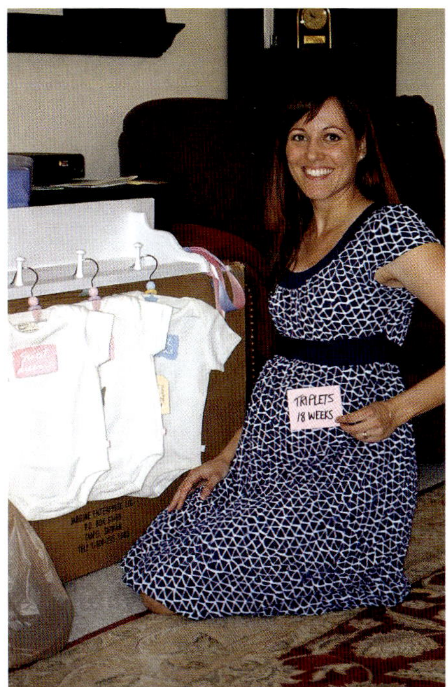


Triplet baby shower at 18 weeks

Time with my little buddy, Johnny, before strict bedrest

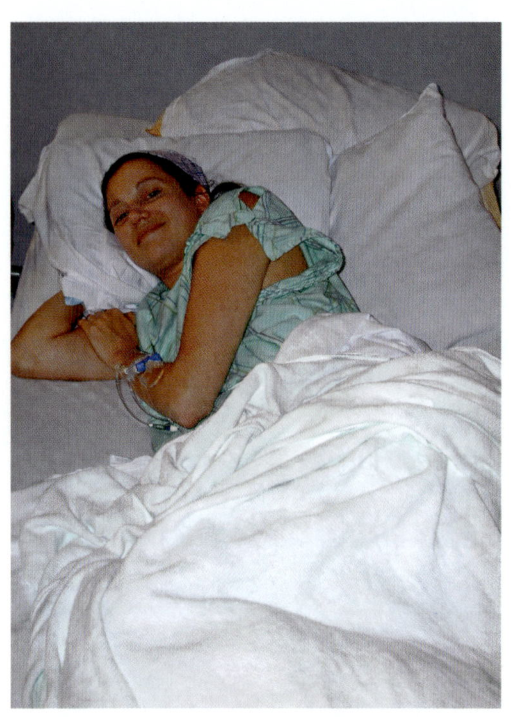

Life in the hospital

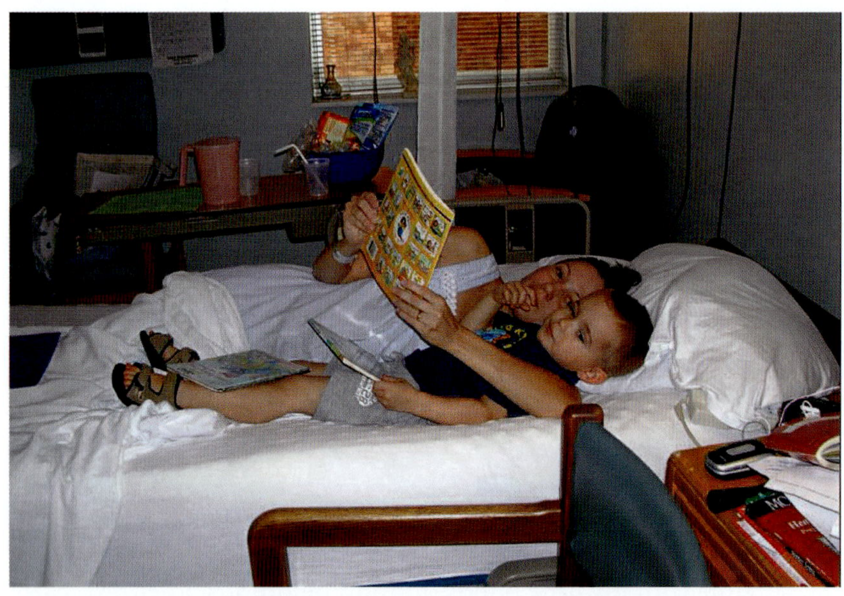

Reading to one of my favorite visitors

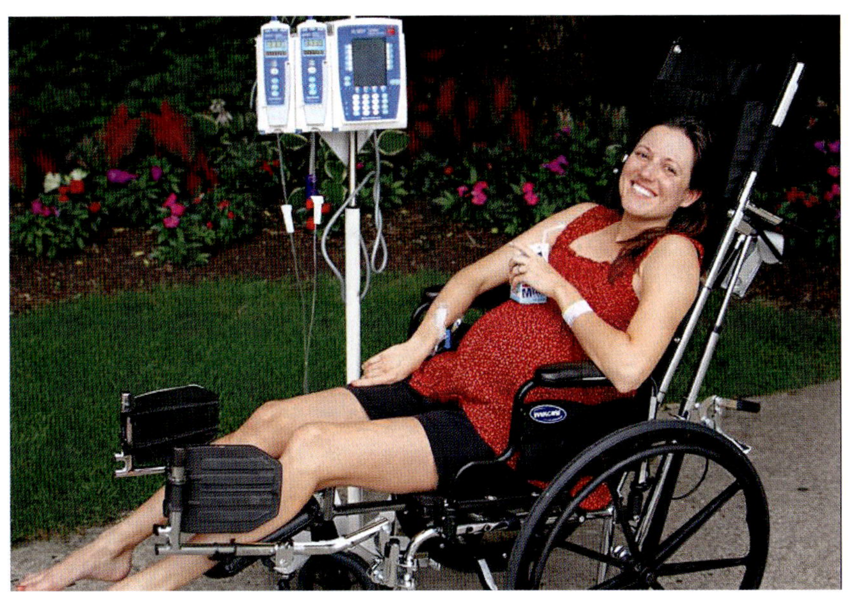

My trip outside on my birthday—just hours before the triplets were born

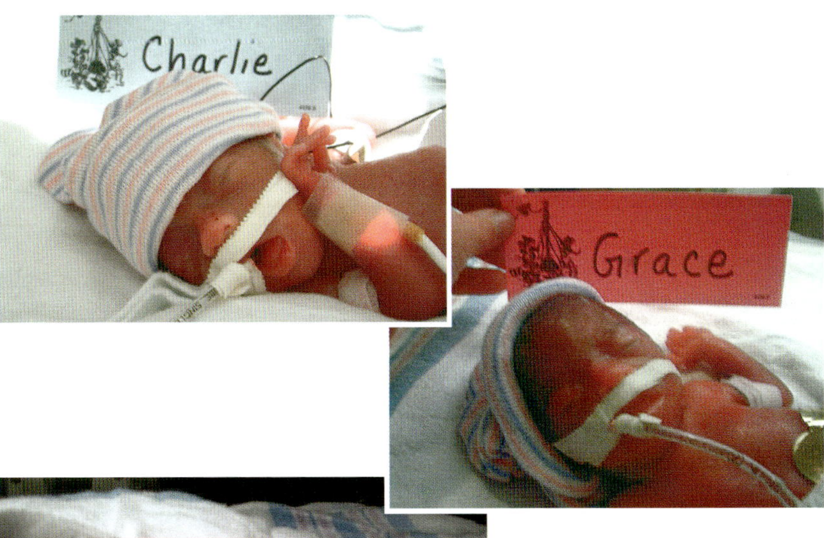


The triplets shortly after being born at 24 weeks—each weighing in at a little over one pound

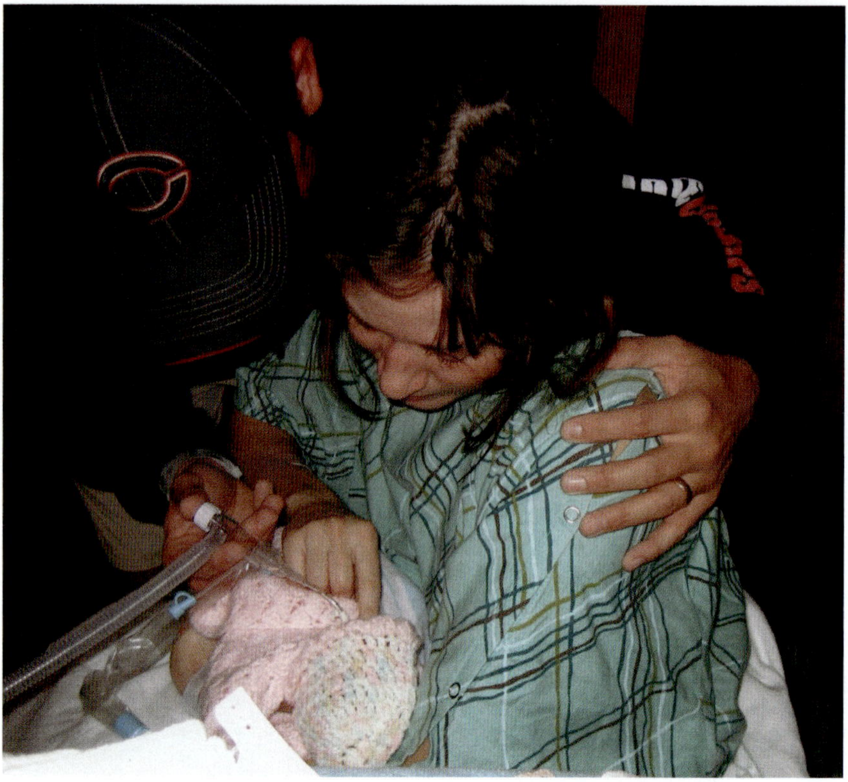

Dave and I holding Grace as she died in my arms

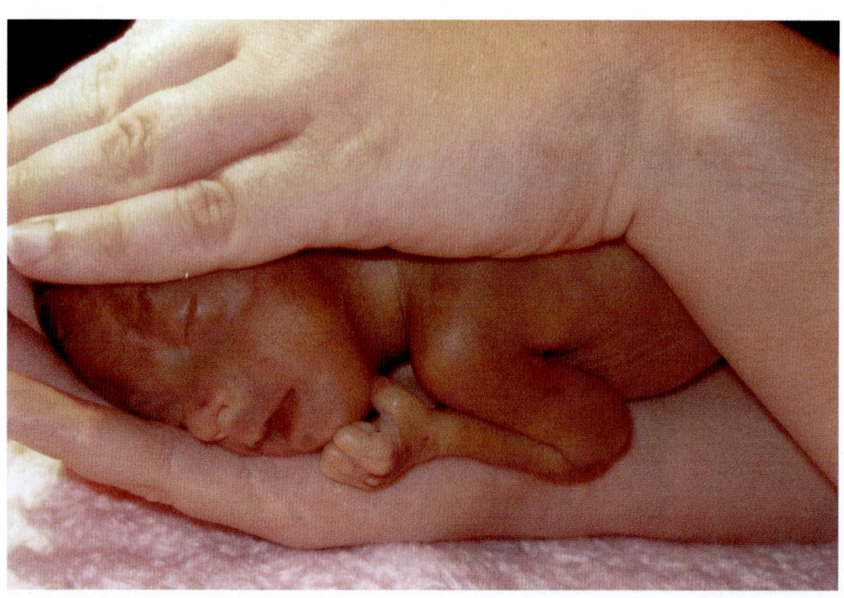

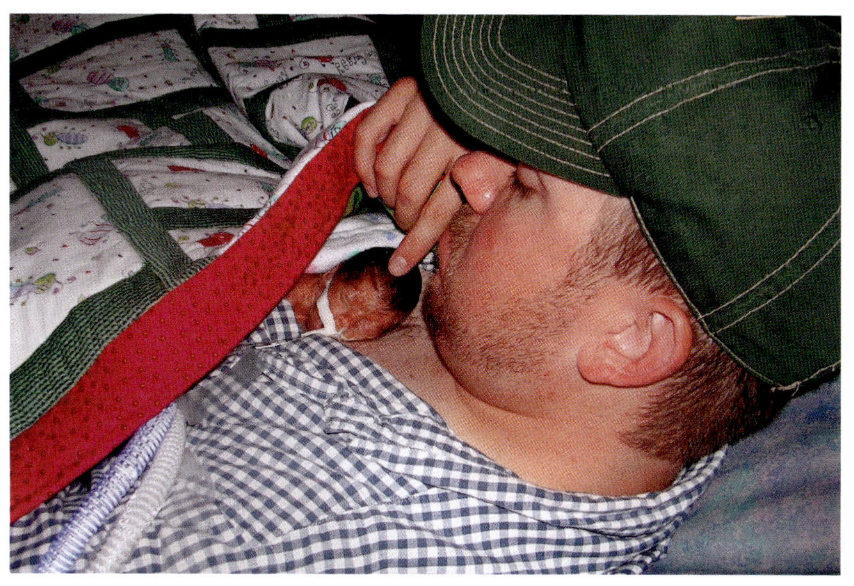

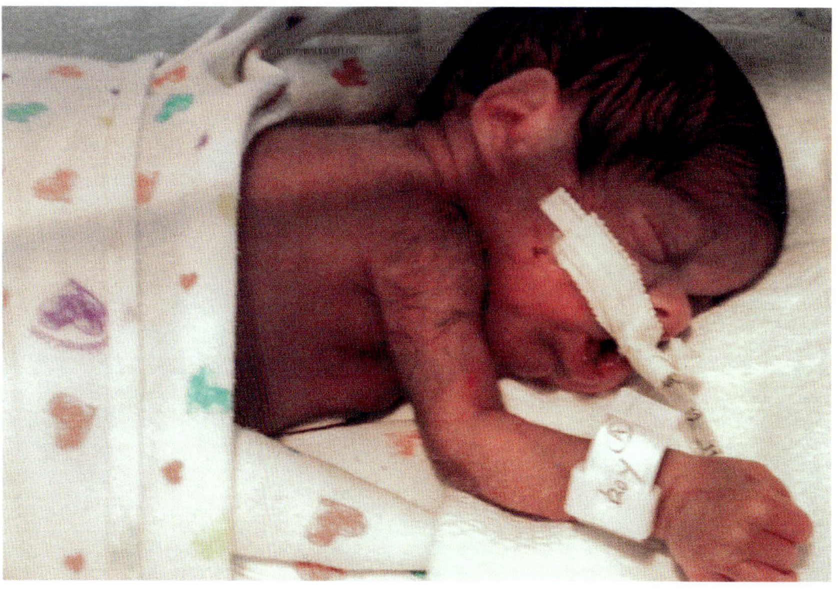

Time with Charlie in the NICU

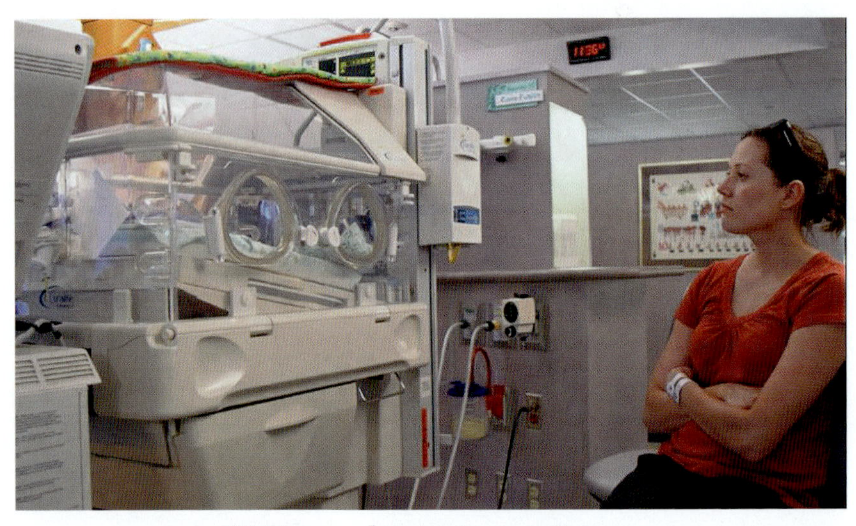

Waiting . . . hoping . . . praying . . .

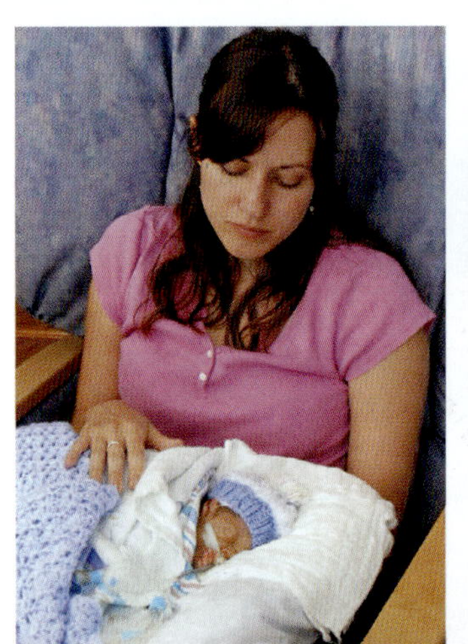

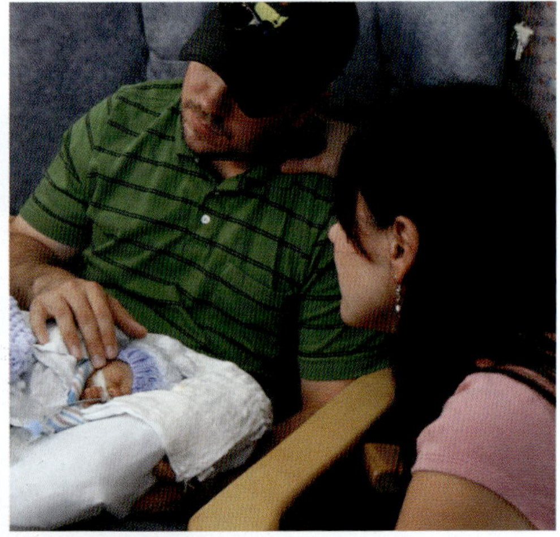

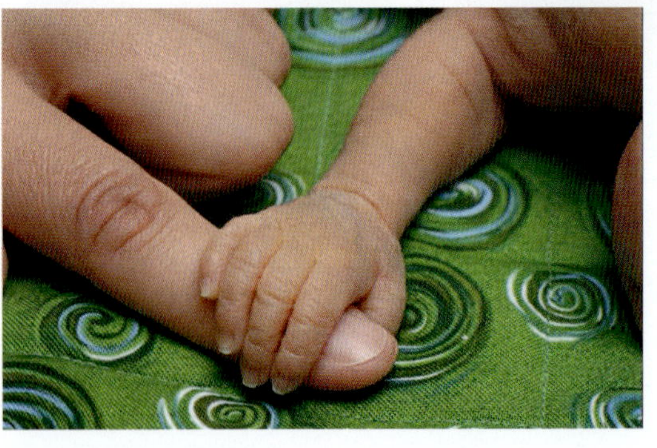

Our last few moments with Charlie . . .

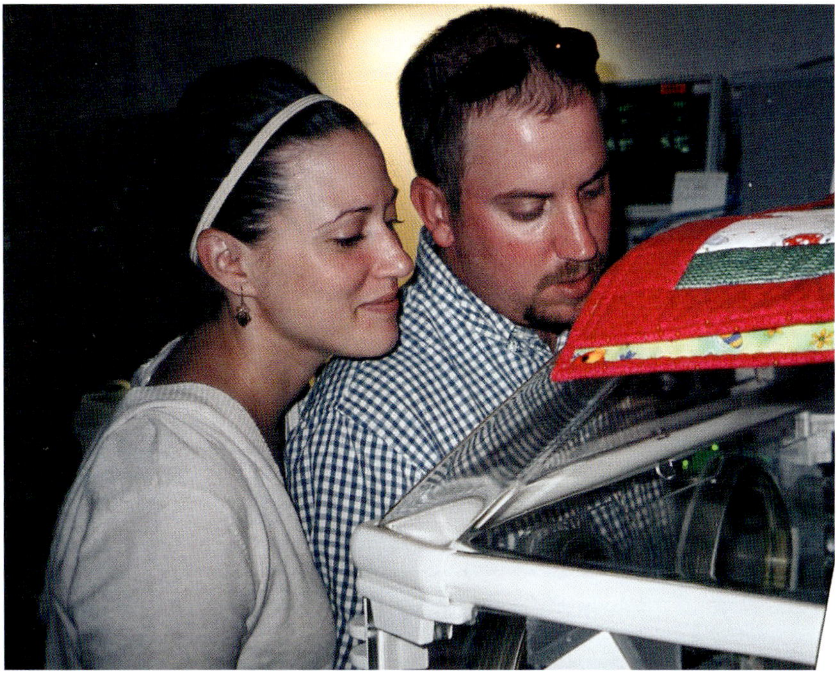

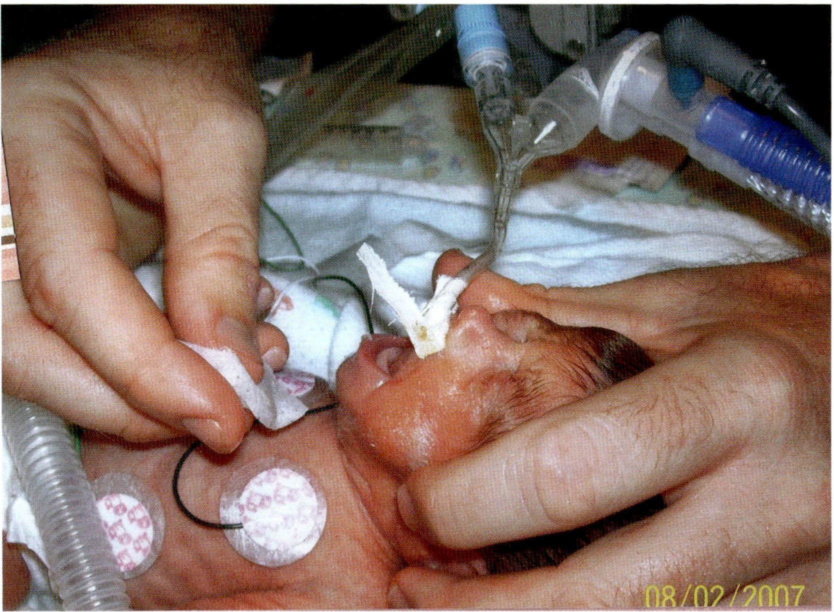


Life in the NICU with Emma Jane

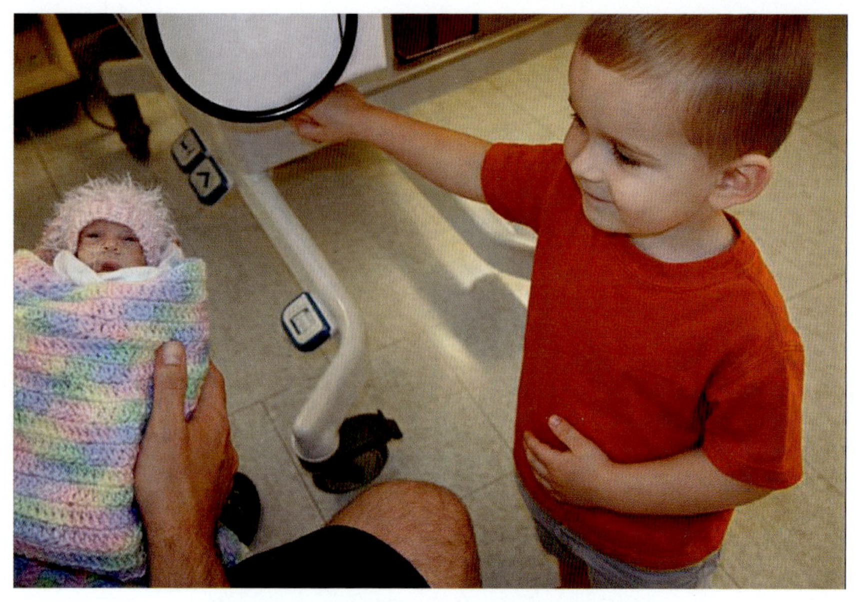

Johnny meets Emma for the first time

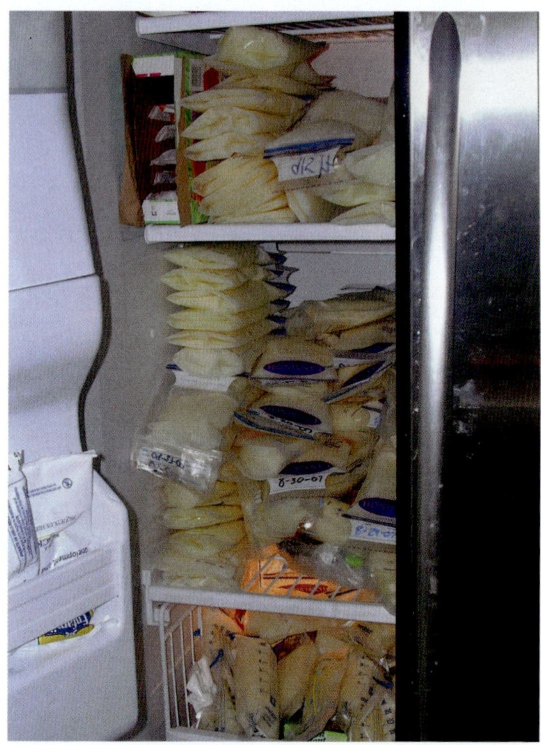


A freezer full of milk

Kangaroo Care

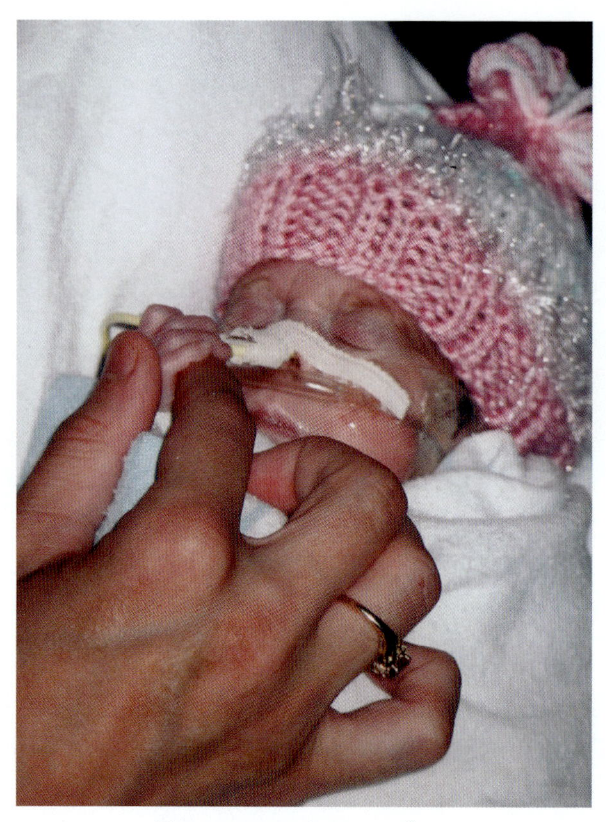

Emma growing steady . . .

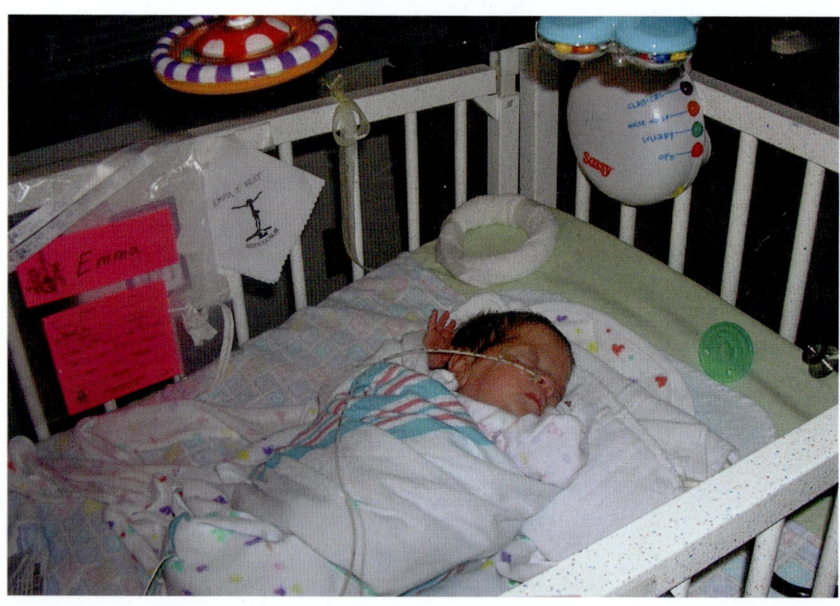

Emma graduates from the NICU and leaves the hospital after 117 days there

Emma's first few months at home with her big brother

Next to my preemie Cabbage Patch doll

Emma and our family through the years . .

Emma holding a picture of herself in the NICU—
now healthy, happy, and fully alive!

A bittersweet moment at the cemetery on one of our birthdays

Me and my miracle baby—at age 16

## *About the Author*

JULIE YOST is a wife and mother who has dedicated her life to serving the Catholic Church in various roles, including high school religion teacher, community service director, and campus minister. She has also volunteered extensively in children's, youth, and women's ministries—teaching classes, leading retreats, and speaking at events.

Julie holds a bachelor's degree in education from the University of Dayton and a master's degree in pastoral ministry from Mount Saint Mary's Seminary in Cincinnati, Ohio. She also completed the two-year program at the Encounter School of Ministry in Cincinnati, where she currently serves as an instructor.

Through enduring the profound loss of children and surviving her own battle with breast cancer, Julie has developed a deep understanding of God's presence amid suffering and His ability to bring about healing and redemption. She is passionate about sharing the hope she's found in her most challenging seasons and loves inspiring others to encounter the Lord during their own times of struggle and hardship.

In her daily life, Julie enjoys spending time with her family and close friends, savoring a hot cup of coffee on her front porch, and singing praises to God loudly in her living room.

To learn more or contact Julie, visit her at www.julieyost.com or follow her on Instagram @julielynnyost.